BIBLICAL STUDIES FROM THE CATHOLIC BIBLICAL ASSOCIATION OF AMERICA

GENERAL EDITOR

SHEILA McGINN
FRANK J. MATERA (Emeritus)

EDITORIAL BOARD

J. E. AGUILAR CHIU • J. ATKINSON
R. BAUTCH • A. HARKINS • P. SPITALER

Previous Volumes in Biblical Studies from the CBA

1.
A Concise Theology of the New Testament
Frank J. Matera

2.
Letters to the Johannine Circle: 1–3 John
Francis J. Moloney, SDB

3.
The Landscape of the Gospels: A Deeper Meaning
Donald Senior, CP

4.
Scripture and Tradition in the Letters of Paul
Ronald D. Witherup, PSS

5.
Christ in the Book of Revelation
Ian Boxall

6.
Come and See: Discipleship in the Gospel of John
Sherri Brown

7.
The Theology and Spirituality of the Psalms of Ascents
Bradley C. Gregory

8.
Amos and Hosea: The Justice and Mercy of God
Katherine H. Hayes

THE SHAPE OF MATTHEW'S STORY

FRANCIS J. MOLONEY, SDB

Biblical Studies
from the Catholic Biblical
Association

No. 9

Paulist Press
New York / Mahwah, NJ

Scripture texts in this work are taken from the New American Bible, revised edition © 2010, 1991, 1986, 1970 Confraternity of Christian Doctrine, Washington, D.C. and are used by permission of the copyright owner. All Rights Reserved. No part of the New American Bible may be reproduced in any form without permission in writing from the copyright owner.

Cover image by Art Posting / Shutterstock.com
Cover design by Dawn Massa, Lightly Salted Graphics
Book design by Lynn Else

Copyright © 2023 by The Catholic Biblical Association

All rights reserved. No part of this publication may be reproduced, stored in a retrieval system, or transmitted in any form or by any means, electronic, mechanical, photocopying, recording, scanning, or otherwise, without either the prior written permission of the Publisher, or authorization through payment of the appropriate per-copy fee to the Copyright Clearance Center, Inc., www.copyright.com. Requests to the Publisher for permission should be addressed to the Permissions Department, Paulist Press, permissions@paulistpress.com.

Library of Congress Cataloging-in-Publication Data
Names: Moloney, Francis J. (Francis James), 1940- author.
Title: The shape of Matthew's story / Francis J. Moloney.
Description: New York : Paulist Press, [2022] | Series: Biblical studies from the Catholic Biblical Association of America ; no. 9 | Includes bibliographical references. | Summary: "Approaching a Gospel as a "story," i.e., a narrative whole, is widely used by contemporary scholarly commentators. But it is not familiar to many audiences. There are several reasons for this. Catholic audiences are accustomed to hearing passages excerpted from one of the four Gospels at Mass, or within the context of other liturgical settings. The location of the passage within the literary whole of the story (its literary context) is seldom recognized. Similarly, there are "favourite passages" that appear regularly: e.g., Peter's confession in Matt 16:13–20 (generally without the narrative conclusion of vv. 21–23), and the final commission of the risen Jesus in 28:16–20. Where do these famous passages come in the story? How are they part of a broader picture of the Gospel's presentation of God and God's action in and through Jesus? The proposed book would focus upon the unfolding of the narrative, section by section, seeking to trace a single-minded presentation of God, Jesus Christ, the call to discipleship and the Christian Church, articulated as the story unfolds"—Provided by publisher.
Identifiers: LCCN 2023001738 (print) | LCCN 2023001739 (ebook) | ISBN 9780809155989 (paperback) | ISBN 9780809187560 (ebook)
Subjects: LCSH: Bible. Matthew—Criticism, interpretation, etc.
Classification: LCC BS2575.52 .M65 2022 (print) | LCC BS2575.52 (ebook) | DDC 226.2/06—dc23/eng/20230721
LC record available at https://lccn.loc.gov/2023001738
LC ebook record available at https://lccn.loc.gov/2023001739

ISBN 978-0-8091-5598-9 (paperback)
ISBN 978-0-8091-8756-0 (e-book)

Published by Paulist Press
997 Macarthur Boulevard
Mahwah, New Jersey 07430
www.paulistpress.com

Printed and bound in the
United States of America

For Brendan, Mary, and Dorothy

Contents

About the Series ix

Preface..xi

Chapter One. Matthew among the Gospels..........................1

Chapter Two. The Coming of the Messiah
    (Matthew 1:1 – 4:16)..14

Chapter Three. Jesus' Ministry of Preaching and
    Healing (Matthew 4:17 – 11:1)......................................25

Chapter Four. The Crisis in the Ministry of the
    Messiah (Matthew 11:2 – 16:23) 44

Chapter Five. The Messiah's Journey to Jerusalem
    (Matthew 16:13 – 20:34)..67

Chapter Six. The Messiah's Death and Resurrection
    in Jerusalem (Matthew 21:1 – 28:15).............................82

Chapter Seven. The Great Commission
    (Matthew 28:16-20)...113

Epilogue: Meticulous Matthew 117

Appendix One: The Shape of Matthew's Story 123

Appendix Two: An Outline of Matthew's Story................127

Select Bibliography 131

About the Series

This series, Biblical Studies from the Catholic Biblical Association of America, seeks to bridge the gap between the technical exegetical work of the academic community and the educational and pastoral needs of the ecclesial community. Combining careful exegesis with a theological understanding of the text, the members of the Catholic Biblical Association of America and those invited by the Association have written these volumes in a style that is accessible to an educated, nonspecialized audience, without compromising academic integrity.

These volumes deal with biblical texts and themes that are important and vital for the life and ministry of the Church. While some focus on specific biblical books or particular texts, others are concerned with important theological themes, still others with archaeological and geographical issues, and still others with questions of interpretation. Through this series, the members of the Catholic Biblical Association of America are excited to present the results of their research in a way that is relevant to an interested audience that goes beyond the confines of the academic community.

Preface

The storytelling nature of Matthew, Mark, Luke, and John is the feature that sets them apart from the other documents in the New Testament. In the decades before the appearance of the Gospels, Paul informed his audiences that he was communicating "good news." He used the Greek expression *euangelion* to communicate that truth to his hearers and listeners (see, e.g., Rom 1:1, 9, 16; 2:16; 10:16; 11:28; 15:16, 19; 16:25). However, since the time of the Gospel of Mark (about 70 CE), the expression "Gospel" has come to refer to a story of Jesus (Mark 1:1: "The beginning of the gospel [*tou euangeliou*] of Jesus Christ, the Son of God").

This study of Matthew's story of Jesus concentrates on the fact that it is a story.[1] This is often forgotten by those who read and hear individual episodes during Christian services. We use favorite Gospel passages without awareness of which Gospel they come from. Stories have a beginning, a middle, and an end. The beginning can be a "prologue" (Matt 1:1–4:16) and the end, a "conclusion" (28:16-20). Between the beginning and the end of a long story, different episodes are placed side by side. In the First Gospel, the deliberate sequence of events, words, actions, reports of positive, negative, and neutral responses to Jesus, is not the result of a random or accidental collection of Jesus stories.

---

1. I will refer to the Gospel as "the First Gospel," and to the unknown author as "Matthew." See W. D. Davies and Dale C. Allison Jr., *The Gospel according to Saint Matthew*, 3 vols., International Critical Commentary (Edinburgh: T. & T. Clark, 1988-1997), 1:7-17.

THE SHAPE OF MATTHEW'S STORY

They were told *in this way* because an early Christian whom we call "Matthew" wanted to communicate "good news" to his audience, to call them to a decision for Jesus Christ.

A necklace is made up of a variety of beautiful stones, perhaps of various shapes and colors. An artist puts them side by side, giving a final shape to the necklace *by means of the thread that unites them*. Stories are shaped in this way. It is not an individual precious stone that makes the necklace beautiful but the production of a unified artistic piece. This is not to deny that some of the stones may stand out and catch the eye of the beholder more than others. The following book traces a "narrative thread" that runs from Jesus' coming as the Messiah (1:1 – 4:16) to an initial ministry (4:17 – 11:1) that creates crisis and division (11:2 – 16:12). He journeys to Jerusalem with his disciples (16:13 – 20:34) and there is crucified and rises from death (21:1 – 28:15). The story ends as the risen Jesus sends his disciples to all nations and promises to be with them till the end of the age (28:16–20).

For many decades, I have been blessed by the wisdom and the regular company of Professors Brendan Byrne, SJ, Dorothy Lee, and Mary Coloe, PBVM. This book is a small token of my gratitude to that company.

CHAPTER ONE

Matthew among the Gospels

Everyone enjoys a good story. This is true for the Gospels of Matthew, Mark, Luke, and John. They are best understood as part of the storytelling tradition of Christians from the first century. Before setting out on a closer reading of Matthew's story of Jesus in the chapters that follow, some more general reflections on the Gospels as stories are called for. This chapter will close with a proposed overall presentation of the literary shape of the Gospel of Matthew. The remaining chapters will delve more deeply into Matthew's meticulous shaping of the various parts of the story that generated his whole utterance.

READING AND HEARING STORIES

A good story addresses the experiences of the audience. As we say, some stories "speak to me." This means that when we read or hear a good story, *we become part of that story*. An author has a passion to communicate with an audience and she or he writes a narrative to communicate that passion. Stories have been part of human communication from time immemorial. Most cultures have long-held foundational stories that communicate their origins, religious truths that they hold dear (god[s], creation, accepted social and ethical behavior, behavior that responds to their god's plan for humankind, and so on), and the lives of their founding heroes. The success or failure of a story does not depend on a historical "author." Sometimes (as is the case with the Gospels) the real author's identity is long since lost. The same must be said for the original audience. *The story itself* contains (or lacks) what is needed for a successful process of communication. The original author and the original audience may be gone, but stories are told and retold.

A narrative reports the interactions of characters, events, descriptions of locations, and the passing of time. This aspect of a narrative can be called the *story*, but narratives communicate something more than *story*: values, hopes, dreams of a better world, the blessings, and tragedies that follow human decisions and interaction. This aspect of a narrative can be called its *discourse*.

> A *story* captures the imagination of an audience by a well-designed reporting of a succession of events and interaction of characters, from beginning to end. It also communicates a message, a *discourse*, challenging the mind and the heart of an audience.

MATTHEW AS A STORY

The historical author of the First Gospel has long since gone, as has his original audience. We do not know anything about the character, the personality, and the psyche of Matthew. Nor can we ask the original audience what the story meant to them. The title "The Gospel according to Matthew" was added to the copies of a Greek original early in the second Christian century. Interpreters have long attempted to identify "Matthew."[1] It appears that he describes himself as a "scribe who has been instructed in the kingdom of heaven (who) is like the head of a household who brings from his treasure both the new and the old" (Matt 13:52).

The most likely reason for the decision of the earliest scribes to declare that this Gospel was "according to Matthew" stems from the conviction of early Christian tradition that one of the Twelve was the author. In his description of Jesus' call of the tax collector to discipleship, Matthew is following the Gospel of Mark. Mark names the tax collector "Levi" (Mark 2:13-17; see Luke 5:27-32), but Matthew reports that Jesus saw "a man named Matthew sitting at the customs post" and called him to become his follower (Matt 9:9).

In the First Gospel's list of the Twelve appointed by Jesus to be with him in a special way in Matthew 10:1-4, Matthew adds a detail not found elsewhere in the lists of the Twelve (see Mark 3:16-19). He rewrites the list, including "Matthew the tax collector" (Matt 10:3a). The conviction that a member of Jesus' chosen "Twelve" (Matt 10:1-4) wrote the First Gospel was founded on an early Christian author's listing one of the Twelve as "Matthew the tax collector" (10:3a). We cannot be sure that Matthew the tax collector was the author of the First Gospel. Mark calls him "Levi" (Mark 2:13-14) but does not list him among the Twelve in 3:16-19. Out of respect for that two-thousand-year-old tradition, we will call our author "Matthew."

Early in the Gospel we become aware that Matthew's story of Jesus attempts to persuade a reader of certain truths about the figure at the center of the narrative. The Gospel's

---

1. See Ulrich Luz, *Matthew*, trans. James E. Crouch, 3 vols., Hermeneia (Minneapolis: Fortress, 2003-2007), 1:59-60.

first page insists that Jesus is the Messiah, the son of David, the son of Abraham (Matt 1:1), son of Abraham (vv. 2–6), son of David (vv. 7–15), and the Messiah (v. 16). For Matthew, the birth of Jesus is the result of a God-directed history of Israel that ran from Abraham to the Messiah, Jesus of Nazareth (1:1–17; see 2:23).

Matthew has strong convictions about the person of Jesus (see 16:13–20; 27:54). He is the new and perfect Moses, giving a new Law to a new people of God (5:1—7:29), a Messiah who brings healing and peace to the afflicted (8:1—9:38), instituting the Twelve (10:1–4) and forming his disciples (16:13—20:34). The Gospel closes with a presentation of the risen Jesus as Lord, promising that he will be with believers until the end of the age (28:16–20).

Matthew seeks to persuade his audience that the traditions of Israel are not destroyed or abandoned; they are "perfected" by Jesus (see 5:17 and 13:52). The leaders of Israel reject this claim. They oppose and reject Jesus, and Jesus condemns them (see 23:13, 15, 27), threatening that the kingdom will be taken away from them (21:42) and that their city will be destroyed (22:7). Matthew's audience encounters these threats in the second half of the 80s of the first Christian century. They are involved in a mission to the Gentiles (20:16–20), and the city of Jerusalem was destroyed by the Romans in 70 CE. For Matthew, the coming of the Messiah challenges the status quo, but not all are willing to accept that Jesus is the Messiah. The First Gospel reflects two scribal traditions: that of Israel with its strong focus on the Torah, and that of Jesus Christ, bringing forth treasures both "new and old" (13:52). Conflict is inevitable.

The story is filled with characters: Jesus, his parents, especially Joseph, John the Baptist, his disciples, a chosen group of "Twelve," a broader group of disciples, the crowds, the Jewish leaders, especially the Pharisees, but also the

Scribes and the Sadducees. There are lesser characters who come and go as the recipients of Jesus' words and actions (e.g., a paralytic, the woman with the flow of blood, a young girl, two blind men, a deaf mute, individual disciples, and especially Simon Peter). The story is played out in various places (Bethlehem, Egypt, the desert, Capernaum, towns and villages, "on the road," and Jerusalem). It unfolds along a timeline: Jesus is born in Bethlehem, initially ministers in Galilee, journeys to Jerusalem as hostility mounts, and dies and rises in the city.

Matthew attempts to engage an audience to persuade that Jesus of Nazareth is the son of Abraham, the son of David, the son of God, the Messiah (1:1-17) who will be with us as our risen Lord till the end of all time (28:16-20). He seeks to involve them in a quality of life that perfects what was required by the Law and the Prophets (5:1 – 8:1a), pointing out that a final judgment will separate the sheep from the goats on the basis of how well they cared for "the least of my brethren" (25:31-46).

> Matthew has written a coherent story to communicate truths that he regarded as fundamental consequences of the coming of Jesus as the Messiah. Christian audiences of the third millennium continue to hear and read Matthew's story as it makes sense of their own story.

MATTHEW, MARK, LUKE, AND JOHN

As the author most likely describes himself as a scribe instructed in the kingdom, drawing out of his storehouse treasures both new and old (13:52), Matthew was most likely an early convert from Judaism to Christianity. A long

THE SHAPE OF MATTHEW'S STORY

tradition associates the origin of the First Gospel in the city of Antioch in Syria. The proximity of this city to Israel enabled the presence of a community of Jews, many perhaps fleeing from the chaos that followed the destruction of Jerusalem in 70 CE. Matthew is probably one of several former members of the synagogue in that city (a scribe) who accepted that Jesus of Nazareth was the Christ (instructed in the kingdom of heaven).

Matthew's story of Jesus was told against the background of tension between two Jewish groups: the Jews of the synagogue in Antioch and the newly established Christian Church in the same city. "Matthew is the *discipled scribe* instructed by his teacher of wisdom on how the new and the old interact."[2] As we trace Matthew's story of Jesus, searching for its perennial meaning for Christians, we must also ask historical questions. What situations in Antioch generated this Gospel, and are reflected in the Jesus' story? The final version of each Gospel story can be described as a *two-level drama*. Matthew's telling of the drama of Jesus' life-story in the 30s of the first Christian century is being told against the background of the drama of the Christian community in the final decades of that century. The portrait of the Jews and their leaders in the First Gospel reflects a time of conflict and perhaps mutual insult, late in the first century, as both Jews and Christians struggled to establish their identities after the destruction of Jerusalem (70 CE).

The following journey through the First Gospel recognizes the narrative nature of the text. It also attempts to identify literary structures that provide the skeleton shaping the flesh of the story. Specialists will correctly remark that such an approach is a type of formalism. I accept that, but literary formalism often brackets out historical circumstances

---

2. Patrick Schreiner, *Matthew, Disciple and Scribe: The First Gospel and Its Portrait of Jesus* (Grand Rapids: Baker Academic, 2019), 4.

that may have played a role in determining the shape of a narrative. History, as well as literary concerns helped shape Matthew's story. Formalists focus intensely on the text. A situation late in the first century, as both Jews and Christians struggled to establish their identities after the destruction of Jerusalem (70 CE), sheds light on the interpretation of a story that most likely first appeared around 85–90 CE.[3]

Products of a modern critical era, it is part of our DNA to accept as "true" only those reported events that can be proven to have happened. We fail to understand the First Gospel if we read or hear it as a modern history book. A succinct statement of the "truth" of the Gospels can be found in paragraph 19 of the Dogmatic Constitution on Divine Revelation (*Dei Verbum*) from the Second Vatican Council. After affirming the close link between the Gospel narratives and what Jesus of Nazareth said and did, the document continues:

> After the ascension of the Lord, the apostles handed on to their hearers what he had said and done, but with that fuller understanding which they, instructed by the glorious events of Christ and enlightened by the Spirit of truth, now enjoyed.

The Council fathers go on to insist on the importance of the story of Jesus, but not as a simple history book. The sacred authors, in writing the four Gospels,

> selected certain of the many elements that had been handed on.... They synthesized or explained with an eye to the situation of the churches. They retained the preaching style, but always in such a

---

3. See Michal Beth Dinkler, *Literary Theory and the New Testament* (New Haven, CT: Yale University Press, 2019), 44–70.

THE SHAPE OF MATTHEW'S STORY

fashion that they have told us *the authentic truth about Jesus*.[4]

The "authentic truth about Jesus" does not depend on the accurate recording of the events of his day-to-day life and ministry, but on a careful selection from early traditions "enlightened by the Spirit of truth."

The Gospels are *proclamations of eternal truths* through the assembly of theologically and christologically inspired stories from the life, teaching, death, and resurrection of Jesus. The people who wrote the Gospels believed, and they wrote them that others might believe. The "shape" of the narrative of the First Gospel is the result of a careful gathering of memories and traditions about Jesus, told to communicate Matthew's understanding of "the authentic truth about Jesus."

> Gospel stories are not primarily history books, even though they contain a great deal of historical reporting from the time of Jesus and the early Church. They are inspired proclamations, in a story form, of what God has done for humankind in and through Jesus of Nazareth. "After the ascension of the Lord, the apostles handed on to their hearers what he had said and done, but with that fuller understanding which they, instructed by the glorious events of Christ and enlightened by the Spirit of truth, now enjoyed." (*Dei Verbum* 19)

It is almost universally agreed that the Gospel of Mark was the first Christian Gospel to appear about 70 CE, closely

---

[4]. Austin Flannery, ed., *Vatican Council II: Constitutions and Declarations; A Completely Revised Translation in Inclusive Language* (Northport, NY: Costello Publications, 2007), 110–11. Italics added.

associated with the Jewish War. The theme of a suffering Messiah dominates the narrative. Some time passed before Matthew and Luke appeared. Matthew strives to show how the newness of Jesus continues and completes God's earlier promises to Israel, while Luke reaches out to a Gentile world with a more universal message.

The evangelist Luke opens his Gospel by informing his audience that "many have undertaken to compile a narrative of the events that have been fulfilled among us" (Luke 1:1). The Gospel of Mark would have been one such narrative. Both Luke and Matthew used the Gospel of Mark as their major source, writing in different circumstances in the second half of the 80s CE. They follow Mark's order of events from the life of Jesus. The Gospels of Mark, Matthew, and Luke can be placed side by side, as they recount the same basic story. They are called the Synoptic Gospels, an expression that indicates our ability to see the three of them with one glance of the eye (Greek: *sun-opsis*).

Matthew and Luke also had other traditions from the life and teaching of Jesus that were not from the Gospel of Mark. Perhaps the best known of these is a long sermon that Jesus delivers on a mountain in the First Gospel (Matt 5:1 – 7:29) and on a level place in Luke (Luke 6:12-49). Modern interpreters have invented a name for the large amount of Jesus-material found only in the First Gospel and the Gospel of Luke. Taking the first letter of the German word for "source" (Quelle), it has been given the name Q. There is no document that contains only Q. Interpreters reconstruct it from what is common to both Matthew and Luke. Then there are words and events that only Matthew reports. He binds together and shapes his sources to reflect his unique (and inspired) point of view.

THE SHAPE OF MATTHEW'S STORY

> Christians must respect the unique theological and Christological *discourse* of each Gospel within the fourfold Gospel tradition. Recognizing that eternal truths are proclaimed by the *stories* of Matthew, Mark, Luke, and John gives Christians access to mutually enriching, inspired instruction on the action of God in Jesus Christ, and a lifestyle that is modelled upon him.

THE SHAPE OF MATTHEW'S STORY

Matthew's association with Israel and Jewish traditions has long been regarded as the reason for five long discourses across the narrative. Many suggest that Matthew regards these five sermons as modeled on the Jewish Torah: the first five books of Israel's Sacred Scriptures. Each of them opens with Jesus' adopting an authoritative teaching role (5:1; 10:1; 13:1–3; 18:1; 23:1) and closes with a formal indication that he had "finished these words" (7:28; see 11:1; 13:53; 19:1; 26:1):

1. The sermon on the mount: 5:1 – 7:29.
2. The sermon on mission: 10:1 – 11:1.
3. The parables sermon: 13:1–53.
4. The sermon on order in the community: 18:1 – 19:1.
5. The sermon on the end of time and final judgment: 23:1 – 26:1.

Using the five sermons as the key to Matthew's literary structure makes it difficult to discern links between the long narratives that precede and follow the sermons. Recent interpreters have argued for the extensive use of triads (material gathered in threes) across both discourses and narratives,[5] but the process seems to slacken halfway through the story. What follows assumes that Matthew shaped a "life-story" that began with Jesus' birth and ended with his death and resurrection. The narrative is framed by a prologue (1:1–4:16) and the great commission (28:16-20).

Matthew blends narrative and discourse to follow Jesus' progress from birth to resurrection.

> *Matthew 1:1–4:16. The Coming of the Messiah.* The infancy narrative (1:1–2:23), the disclosure of the identity of Jesus by the Baptist, and his "testing" by Satan (3:1–4:16) function as a "prologue" to the Gospel.
>
> *Matthew 4:17–11:1. Jesus' Ministry of Preaching and Healing.* Summary statements on Jesus' preaching and healing (4:23; 9:35; 11:1), associated with his preaching (5:1–7:28) and healing ministry (8:1–9:37), are interlaced with discipleship material. The mission of Jesus is passed on to the disciples (10:1–11:1).
>
> *Matthew 11:2–16:23. The Crisis in the Ministry of the Messiah.* Jesus' person and role are further revealed, but the leaders of Israel reject him. Across 11:2–14:12 intercalated presentations of the rejection and affirmation of Jesus calls the audience to decision. Jesus establishes a new "family" (11:2–12:50). The parables of Jesus punish the hard-heartedness of Israel and bless disciples. Jesus' hometown rejects him (13:1-58). Disciples are associated with Jesus' ministry (14:1-35), as Israel continues to fail (15:1-20), leading to more demonstrations of Jesus' authority (15:21-39) and further rejection (16:1-12). The section closes with Peter's confession of Jesus

---

5. Davies and Allison, *Saint Matthew*, 58-72.

THE SHAPE OF MATTHEW'S STORY

at Caesarea Philippi, and his refusal to accept that Jesus must suffer, die, and rise again (16:13-28).

Matthew 16:13 – 20:34. The Messiah's Journey to Jerusalem. The confession of Peter (16:13-28) acts as a "bridge narrative" from 11:2 – 16:23 into 16:13 – 20:34 that closes with a matching confession of the blind men at Jericho (20:29-34). Jesus predicts his passion and death three times (16:19-28; 17:22-23; 20:17-19). As Jesus journeys to Jerusalem, he forms disciples and instructs them on the challenges that face his "Church."

Matthew 21:1 – 28:15. The Messiah's Death and Resurrection in Jerusalem. Jesus comes to Jerusalem, is rejected (21:1-17; see vv. 15-16), and hostility develops further (23:139). Jesus instructs on the end of Jerusalem and the end of the world (24:1 – 25:46). Throughout the passion story (27:1 – 28:15), Matthew intercalates positive and negative presentations of Jesus and his followers (men and women) to call the audience to decision. Jesus' death and resurrection is "the turning point of the ages."

Matthew 28:16-20. The Great Commission. The risen Jesus' final commission presents God's design for Israel in the universal mission of the Church, and the never-ending presence of the risen Jesus within the community.

Matthew uses a prologue, summary statements, inclusions, repetitions, parallels, triads, chiasms, intercalations, and other literary features to capture and focus his audience's attention.

> Matthew has told his story carefully, looking to the Gospel of Mark, another source (Q), and collecting other traditions that we find only in the First Gospel. He opens his story with

a prologue (1:1—4:16). The body of the narrative follows Jesus' mission in Galilee (4:17—11:1) and the hostility that it creates (11:2—16:12). He turns his face to Jerusalem, instructing his disciples as they journey together (16:13—20:34). There he is crucified and is raised (20:25—28:15). The risen Jesus commissions his disciples to go out to the whole world, promising them he will be with them until the end of the age (28:16-20). The end looks back to the beginning: "They shall name him Emmanuel, which means 'God is with us'" (1:23).

Chapter Two

The Coming of the Messiah

Matthew 1:1 – 4:16

The Gospels contain two birth and infancy narratives (Matt 1–2; Luke 1–2). Matthew 1–2 is somber: a genealogy, the suspicion of an illegitimate birth, the threat of Herod, the slaying of the innocents, the flight into Egypt, and a return home that calls for a further flight to Nazareth because of the threat of another wicked king. Luke 1–2 is more joyful. It provides us with our Christmas pageantry: two annunciations, Mary's visitation to Elizabeth, the birth and naming of John the Baptist and Jesus, the presentation, and the finding of Jesus in the temple. As well as the stories of Jesus' infancy, Matthew and Luke continue their introduction to the person and mission of Jesus with reports of the ministry of John the Baptist, including the account of the baptism of Jesus (Matt 3:1–4:16; Luke 3:1–4:13).

Both Matthew and Luke open Jesus' ministry by reporting the beginning of his preaching (Matt 4:17; Luke 4:14–15). Matthew 1:1–4:16 is addressed directly to the hearer and the reader of the story. In his first pages, Matthew affirms Jesus' divine origins, his status as Son of God and Savior, his "testing" by Satan, and the shadow of the rejection that lies ahead. As Jesus' ministry begins in 4:17, the hearers and the readers of Matthew's story have been left in no doubt about who Jesus Christ is, his origins and his destiny.

THE FUNCTION OF A PROLOGUE

The first pages of all four Gospels introduce the reader and the audience to the person of Jesus, the hero of the narrative that follows, even though Mark 1:1–13 and John 1:1–18 do not tell stories of Jesus' birth and infancy. Authors of all ages have used "prologues" to introduce the hero of a story. In the fifth century BCE, the Greek dramatist Sophocles wrote *Oedipus Rex*. The play opens as a choir informs the audience that Oedipus, a wise and powerful king of Thebes, despite all his efforts to avoid a frightening prophecy, finds that he has slain his father, Laius, and married his mother, Jocasta. She commits suicide by hanging, and Oedipus blinds himself with a pin from her dress. The tragedy is relentless, made even more so by the fact that the audience knows from the outset that Oedipus' worst fears would eventuate. What the audience does not know is *how* the tragedy will unfold. They discover that by following the action of the drama till its final despairing moment when the choir informs the audience that only death reveals the true nature of a human being.

A prologue informs an audience *who* the hero is, and *what* he is destined to do. Only the audience has this knowledge. The characters *in the story* do not share in the knowledge of the audience. This situation places the audience in a *privileged situation* as readers and hearers of the events that follow. In the First Gospel, on arrival at Matthew 4:16, the audience has been informed of the origins of Jesus (1:1–23), his mission and destiny (2:1–23), and of his status as Messiah and Son of God (3:1—4:16). Although the dark shadows that loom across Matthew 1—2 already indicate to the audience that tragedy and rejection lie ahead, they must read the story to its end to trace *how* that happens, *how* tragedy and rejection is resolved, and what that promises for the future.

As Matthew's story unfolds, Jesus proclaims the coming of the kingdom of heaven, is accepted by some, but rejected by the leaders of Israel. The characters in the story: the Twelve, the disciples, the Jewish leaders, the Romans, the crowds, and the individual characters who play cameo roles from time to time, have not heard or read the prologue. The Twelve and the disciples fail to commit unconditionally to Jesus and his mission, and are judged "of little faith," the crowds cannot decide, and the leaders of Israel, in collusion with Roman authorities, execute Jesus. God raises him from death. The audience is called to decision. Whose side are they on: Jesus and those who accept him as the Christ, and the kingdom of heaven he proclaims, or those who reject and slay him?

MATTHEW 1:1 – 4:16: PROLOGUE TO MATTHEW'S STORY OF JESUS

Matthew's infancy story tells of the genealogy of Jesus (1:1–17), the way Jesus was born (1:18–23), the coming of the "magi from the east" (2:1–12), the flight into Egypt, and the return to Nazareth (2:13–23). Matthew has selected these accounts from the many traditions that circulated concerning Jesus' birth and infancy to inform his audience about Jesus' origins and destiny. He focuses on the person of Jesus: who he is, and what he will do.

The same can be said for the series of events reported in 3:1 – 4:16. Following the timeline of the Gospel of Mark, and expanding on it, Matthew reports the preaching of John the Baptist (3:1–12; see Mark 1:1–8), the baptism of Jesus

(3:13-17; see Mark 1:9-11), the devil's testing of Jesus' sonship (4:1-11; see Mark 1:12-13), and his settling in Capernaum (4:12-16; see Mark 1:14). The prologue of 1:1—4:16 closes as Jesus begins his public ministry (4:17; see Mark 1:15). It opens (1:1; see Gen 22:18) and closes (4:13-16) hinting at a mission to the Gentiles: Jesus is the son of Abraham, the father of the nations (1:1; see Gen 22:18), light to the Gentiles (4:15-16).

Where from and Where to: Matthew 1:1 – 2:23

Solemnly introduced (1:1), Jesus comes onto the stage as the last born in a genealogical sequence that runs from Abraham, through David, to the Messiah (1:1-17). His birth is the result of a God-designed history: a threefold repetition of fourteen generations (v. 17). The following story reflects God's point of view.[1] "Jesus who is called the Messiah" is born of Mary, rather than fathered by Joseph, the male descendent of David (v. 16). An explanation for that strange conclusion to a typically Jewish genealogy is provided in 1:18-25, introduced by verse 18: "This is how the birth of Jesus Christ came about." The consequences of the advent of "magi from the east," wise interpreters of signs in the sky, who came to worship a newborn king of the Jews (2:1-12), are tragic (vv. 13-23).[2] Herod's violent slaying of the male children in Bethlehem (vv. 16-18) forces a flight to Egypt (vv. 13-15), and a subsequent flight to Nazareth as a further wicked king has replaced Herod (vv. 19-23). His own people have rejected Jesus, while Gentiles come to

---

1. The number 14 might be the numerical value of the consonants of "David" in Hebrew. Jesus would be the third (perfect) product of the Davidic line.

2. The biblical background to the rising of a messianic star in the east comes from the prophecy of Balaam (see Num 24:15-24; see especially v. 17).

THE SHAPE OF MATTHEW'S STORY

worship him. Major themes from the Gospel story are foreshadowed.

The infancy narrative of Matthew's story tells of Jesus' origins (Abraham, David, Joseph, and Mary [1:1, 16]), "through the holy Spirit," [v 20], at Bethlehem [2:4–6], and finally from Nazareth [v. 23]). A son of Abraham, he is a true Israelite, but as son of Abraham he is linked with the patriarchal figure in whom all nations will gain blessings (Gen 12:1–4; 22:18). Mary is the fifth of five remarkable women, some of whom are Gentile and others under a shadow of sexual misbehavior, who have made courageous decisions to enable the continuation and the very existence of Israel (Tamar [1:3], Rahab [v. 5], Ruth [v. 5], the wife of Uriah [v. 6], Mary [v. 16]). Jesus' story will involve the Gentile world and those broken by sin. Joseph's acceptance of Mary's son makes Jesus a son of David, born in the city of David (2:5–6).

Joseph's repeated unconditional obedience to instructions from an angel of the Lord makes him a model and upright agent in God's design (1:20–25; 2:13–15, 19–23), a stark contrast to the destructive rejection of Herod and "all Jerusalem" (see 2:3). An angel instructs Joseph to name the child "Jesus" (which means "Yhwh saves"). "He will save his people from their sins" (1:21; see 20:28; 26:28). Joseph obediently names the child "Jesus" (v. 25). He will be the promised Emmanuel, "God with us" (vv. 22–23). The shadow of the violent Herod hints that the hero of the story will suffer. "All Jerusalem" joined Herod's disturbance at the announcement of another king (2:3). They will again be troubled when he arrives in Jerusalem at the end of his story (21:10–11).

There are hints of a relationship with Moses. Moses' birth was accompanied by the slaying of innocent Hebrew male children (Exod 1:15–16). The flight into Egypt leads to the fulfillment of a prophecy that referred to the Exodus: "Out of Egypt I called my son" (2:15; Hosea 11:1). Matthew insists that his birth and subsequent experiences fulfill Israel's Scriptures (1:22–23; 2:5–6; 2:15, 17, 23). The promises made to Israel are coming to their fulfillment. The birth of this child is a turning point in God's relationship with God's people.

Jesus was born in the Davidic city of Bethlehem (2:5–6), but the flight to Egypt, and then to Nazareth ensures that "he shall be called a Nazorean" (2:23). The geographical origins of Jesus of Nazareth bring all the Scriptures to fulfillment. His being called a Nazorean suggests that he is the promised *neser*, the messianic fruit of Jesse, the father of David (see Isaiah 11:1; Matt 1:6).

> A genealogy, the obedient decision of Joseph to accept the pregnant Mary as his wife, the coming of the Magi to worship a newly born king, the violent reaction of King Herod, the flight to Egypt and a subsequent return to Israel, calling for a further flight to Nazareth, is a good story. The audience rises from 1:1—2:23 aware that Jesus is the Christ, the Son of Abraham, the Davidic Messiah (1:1–17), born of the Holy Spirit (vv. 18–20). "Jesus" will save his people (v. 21). He is the Emmanuel (v. 23), king of the Jews (2:2), a shepherd king (2:5–6) worshipped at his birth by Gentiles (vv. 10–11), threatened by death as an infant (vv. 16–18), and a new Moses figure (vv. 14–15). Jesus the Nazorean (v. 23) is the fulfillment of Israel's Sacred Scriptures (1:22–23; 2:5–6; 2:15, 17, 23).

JESUS' MESSIANIC STATUS AFFIRMED AND TESTED: MATTHEW 3:1 – 4:16

The advent of the adult Jesus (3:13) is prefaced by a description of the person and the activity of John the Baptist. He announces the imminent coming of the kingdom of heaven (3:1–2). His "appearance" (v. 1) is part of God's design. The dress, the diet, and the location of John the Baptist's ministry recall the austere prophet Elijah (vv. 1, 4; see 2 Kings 1:8). Matthew introduces Jesus, and the imminent coming of the kingdom of heaven (3:2), through the agency of John the Baptist. Jesus' "appearance" is also God's design (v. 13). This impression is vindicated as he is described as the fulfillment of Isaiah 40:3. Isaiah's prophecy referred to God's action in the return of Israel to their own land after the Babylonian exile. Matthew uses the passage to refer to the coming of Jesus as "the Lord" (*ho kyrios*), the Greek expression used in the LXX to refer to the God of Israel (Matt 3:3).[3]

John's preaching attracts everyone (v. 5). But his fierce words are addressed to the Pharisees and the Sadducees. The coming of Jesus will bring a fiery judgment on these *false* children of Abraham, a "brood of vipers," called to repentance (vv. 7–11). John summons them to a baptism of water that will indicate repentance and conversion. The times are urgent. Someone "greater" is coming; his baptism will bring two consequences: the gift of the Holy Spirit, and a destructive judgment of fire. Jesus is "the greater one" who has authority to communicate the holy spirit of God. Even a God-sent prophet like John is unworthy of performing the most menial of tasks: carry his sandals (v. 11). John calls to repentance and conversion (3:1, 7–11), but Jesus brings salvation (1:21, 25). John the Baptist's preaching and warnings fall on deaf ears, but his person and message make clear, at the beginning of the story, that a new era is broached.

The adult Jesus comes from Galilee to be baptized by John. The Baptist insists that he is not worthy to baptize Jesus (v. 14). Jesus replies, "Allow it for now, for thus it is

---

3. The Septuagint, indicated by the abbreviation LXX, is the pre-Christian Greek translation of Israel's Scriptures.

fitting for us to fulfill all righteousness" (v. 15). Jesus indicates that there is a time of this encounter between Jesus and John the Baptist "now," and a "not yet" when "all righteousness" will be established. That time lies in the future. Now the rites and traditions of Israel must be practiced and fulfilled (see 5:17–18). Jesus' future response to God in his death and resurrection will begin a new era, an era of "all righteousness."

As Jesus emerges from the waters of the Jordan River, the heavens open (v. 16a). In a world where God abides above the firmament and the human story takes place below, the opening of the heavens promises a communication from above (see Gen 7:11; Isa 24:18; Ezek 1:1; Mark 1:10; John 1:51; Rev 4:1; 11:19). There is a visual and an aural aspect to the heavenly communication. John the Baptist *sees* the descent of the Holy Spirit in the appearance of a dove descending upon Jesus (v. 16b), and he *hears* a voice from above proclaiming, "This is my beloved Son, with whom I am well pleased" (v. 17). Divine authority sends the Holy Spirit upon Jesus, enabling him to administer the Spirit, already promised in John the Baptist's description of Jesus' ministry in 3:11. A voice from heaven claims that Jesus is his beloved Son, in whom God is well pleased. The presentation of the person and authority of Jesus climaxes in the proclamation that Jesus is the beloved Son of God (v. 17).

The final episode reported in Matthew's prologue, the so-called temptation of Jesus (4:1–16), is a consequence of the divine declaration at the baptism that he is the Son of God (3:17). Jesus is now directed by the Spirit into the ambiguity of the desert to be "tested" by the devil. After forty days of fasting in preparation for this encounter (see Gen 7:1–24; Exod 24:18; 34:27–28; 1 Kgs 19:1–21; Jonah 3:1–10), the devil approaches, seeking to show that the voice from heaven was wrong.

THE SHAPE OF MATTHEW'S STORY

The key to the episode is the devil's twofold use of the words, "If you are the Son of God" (vv. 3, 6). The devil tries to subordinate the person declared "the Son of God" in 3:17. Responding to these attempts, Jesus cites from Deuteronomy 6–8 (vv. 4, 7, 10). Moses communicated Israel's fundamental commandment (see Deut 6:1: "the commandment") in the famous "Hear, O Israel" of Deuteronomy 6:4-6: the Lord alone is Israel's God; unconditional love and service are due only to the Lord God. In Deuteronomy 6–11, Moses instructs Israel on the commandments that must be obeyed if they wish to be children of God, along with their children, and their children's children (6:2). Within that literary setting, Deuteronomy 6–8 recalls Israel's unfaithfulness in the desert, explaining why Israel wandered for forty years. Passages from Deuteronomy 6–8 provide the words of God for Jesus. Unlike the Exodus generation, God's Son observes them.

The devil commands Jesus to turn stones into bread, but Jesus responds with words from Deuteronomy 8:3: "One does not live by bread alone, but by every word that comes forth from the mouth of God." The Son of God is led by the word of God, not the command of the devil (vv. 3–4). Commanding Jesus to cast himself down from the parapet of the temple, the devil has recourse to Israel's Scriptures, citing Psalm 91:11-12 (vv. 5–6). Jesus returns to Deuteronomy and the commandments that direct the children of Israel: "You shall not put the Lord your God to the test" (Deut 6:16; v. 7). Promised the splendor of the world and creation if he will prostrate himself and worship Satan, Jesus drives away Satan (v. 9: "Get away, Satan"), returning to a command from Deuteronomy: "The Lord, your God, shall you worship and him alone shall you serve" (Deut 6:13; vv. 8–10). The devil leaves the scene, and Jesus is cared for by angels, as is fitting for a Son of God. "Jesus recapitulates the history

The Coming of the Messiah

of God's covenant Son, Israel; but he proves true at the very points where Israel failed: hunger (Exod 16), testing God's faithfulness (Exod 17), and idolatry (Exod 32)."[4]

Hearing that John the Baptist has been arrested, Jesus leaves his known place of origin, Nazareth (see 2:23), and settles at Capernaum in Galilee. Jesus' location in Galilee of the Gentiles (Matt 4:15; LXX Isa 8:23) marks a new era. The light of universal salvation dawns: "The people who sit in darkness have seen a great light, on those dwelling in a land overshadowed by death light has risen" (v. 16; LXX Isa 9:1). The star that led the Gentile wise men to seek Jesus (Matt 2:2, 9–10) will become a light for all who find themselves in darkness (4:16).

The appearance of John the Baptist fulfills the promises of Israel's Scripture (3:3; see Isa 40:3). When John the Baptist is arrested, that era closes, and another begins. The era of Jesus of Nazareth, now settled in Capernaum, continues God's design for all humankind. It also fulfills Israel's Scripture (4:15–16; see LXX Isa 8:23 – 9:1). Jesus' arrival in "Galilee of the Gentiles" (4:14–16) looks back to the proclamation of Jesus as the son of David (1:1), the four women in the genealogy (1:1–17), and the coming of the Magi (2:1–12). Gentiles appear at the beginning, the end, and throughout the prologue to the First Gospel.

> John the Baptist announces Jesus as "the Lord" (3:3), and the mightier one (v. 11a). Jesus will give the Holy Spirit and exercise a fiery judgment (v. 11b–12). His coming broaches a new era, during which all righteousness will be fulfilled (vv. 13–15). He possesses the Holy Spirit and is declared the Son of God by a voice from heaven (vv. 16–17). This claim is

---

4. David E. Garland, *Reading Matthew: A Literary and Theological Commentary on the First Gospel* (New York: Crossroad, 1993), 38.

THE SHAPE OF MATTHEW'S STORY

tested by the devil, but God's Son fulfills the Mosaic requirements for the children of God (4:1-11), and the prophecy that a saving light is dawning among the Gentiles (vv. 15-16). God's promises to Israel are fulfilled in the coming of Jesus Christ (1:1-17, 22-23; 2:5-6, 15, 17-18, 23; 3:3; 4:4, 7, 10, 13-16).

CHAPTER THREE

Jesus' Ministry of Preaching and Healing

Matthew 4:17 – 11:1

As Jesus begins his ministry, he repeats the proclamation of John the Baptist (3:2): "From that time on Jesus began to preach and say, 'Repent, for the kingdom of heaven is at hand'" (4:17).[1] However, John the Baptist was introduced with the words "in those days," a formula regularly used to mark critical moments in God's intervention in history. As Jesus appears actively in the story, "from that time on" God's intervention is further present in Jesus. Crucial elements in that intervention shape this stage of Matthew's story: Jesus calls disciples (4:17-25), delivers a programmatic sermon (5:1 – 8:1a), and works a series of nine miracles (8:1b-17; 8:23 – 9:8; 9:18-34), interspersed with Jesus' instruction of his disciples (8:18-22; 9:9-17; 9:35 – 11:1).

---

1. The Jewish Matthew prefers the expression "the kingdom of heaven" to the "kingdom of God." He uses "Kingdom of God" four times (12:28; 19:24; 21:31, 43).

THE SHAPE OF MATTHEW'S STORY

MATTHEW 4:17–25: THE CALL OF THE FIRST DISCIPLES AND THE BEGINNING OF JESUS' MINISTRY

Jesus summons Simon Peter, Andrew (v. 18), James, and John (v. 21) away from their nets, their boats, and even their father (vv. 20, 22). They are to walk with Jesus, authorized to fish for people (v. 19). As in Elijah's call of Elisha in 2 Kings 19:19–21, they leave all that could be regarded as the signs of their success, to follow him (v. 22). Jesus' ministry opens with his authoritative establishing a discipleship that depends on him entirely. Matthew's reporting Jesus' call of disciples as the very first episode of his ministry is important. It betrays Matthew's concern for the Christian disciples receiving this story of Jesus. "The disciples in the Gospel… are a bridge between the narrative world of the Gospel and the disciples of Matthew's own community."[2]

Matthew articulates two major aspects of Jesus' ministry by a summary: "He went around all of Galilee, teaching in their synagogues, proclaiming the gospel of the kingdom, and curing every disease and illness among the people" (4:23). After a description of the growth of his fame, the breadth of his curing ministry, and the enthusiastic following they generate (vv. 24–25), the first part of the summary ("proclaiming the gospel of the kingdom") is enacted in 5:1—8:1a: Jesus delivers his first discourse, the Sermon on the Mount. He proclaims the good news of the kingdom. Immediately following this discourse, the second aspect of the summary of 4:23 is fulfilled: "curing every disease and illness among the people." Matthew reports a series of nine miracles (8:1—9:38). As that series of events draws to

---

2. Donald Senior, *Matthew*, Abingdon New Testament Commentaries (Nashville: Abingdon Press, 1998), 64.

a close, Matthew frames 5:1—9:38 by repeating his earlier summary: "Then Jesus went around to all the towns and villages, teaching in their synagogues, proclaiming the gospel of the kingdom, and curing every disease and illness" (9:35; see 4:23). On arrival at 10:1, the audience has experienced the challenges of Jesus' teaching (5:1—8:1a) and the power of his healing (8:1b—9:38). The literary frame of 4:23 and 9:35 marks the portrait of Jesus as an authoritative preacher and miracle worker. His discourse on the mission of the Church (10:1—11:1) is also framed by reference to the Twelve (10:1-4; 11:1).

The Overall Shape of Matthew 4:17—11:1: Jesus' Words, Deeds, and Disciples

Frame: Jesus and disciples (4:17-25). Summary of the ministry in Galilee (4:23)
   The Sermon on the Mount (5:1—8:1a)
   Nine miracles and discipleship (8:1b—11:1)
Frame: Jesus and disciples (9:35-38). Summary of the ministry in Galilee (9:35)
Frame: Jesus institutes the Twelve (10:1-4)
   The sermon on mission (10:5-42)
Frame: Jesus completes his instruction of the Twelve (11:1)

MATTHEW 5:1 – 8:1A: THE SERMON ON THE MOUNT

Luke 6:20-49 provides the closest parallel to Matthew's Sermon on the Mount. It is briefer and more urgent. This is an example of traditions shared by Matthew and Luke that we call "Q."[3] Matthew has also used other traditions from Jesus' teaching ministry to provide an instruction to disciples of all times.[4]

The Shape of Matthew 5:1—8:1a: The Sermon on the Mount

Introduction (5:3-16)
    Entrance to the discourse (5:17-20)
        Discourse proper (5:21—7:11)
    Exit from the discourse (7:12)
Conclusion (7:13-27)

Matthew has used the literary practice called a "chiasm" (also called "intercalation") to shape his report of the Sermon on the Mount. The expression comes from the X-shape of the Greek letter *chi* (thus, chi-asm). An author distributes material in such a way that the argument descends from one point to another until it arrives at a central statement. That statement stands alone. Exiting the central statement, the argument ascends, recapturing material that parallels what was said in the descent.

The discourse opens and closes (5:1-2 and 7:28—8:1) with a description of its setting (5:1-2) and its results (7:28—8:1a). These passages can be called sections A and A[1] of the chiastic structure. They are followed and preceded by instructions on the kingdom of heaven, sections B (5:3-16) and B[1] (7:13-27). Two brief statements referring to the Law

---

3. Luke's more universally oriented sermon is delivered on a level place. Matthew's focus is on Moses' traditions.
4. On the Sermon as instruction for all disciples of Jesus, see Frank J. Matera, *The Sermon on the Mount: The Perfect Measure of the Christian Life* (Collegeville, MN: Liturgical Press, 2013).

Jesus' Ministry of Preaching and Healing

and the Prophets serve as C (5:17-20) and C^1 (7:12). They lead into and out of the main body of the discourse. Instruction on the role and importance of possessions, asking when in need, and right judging is stated and restated in 5:21-48 (D) and 6:19-71 (D^1), leading into and exiting the turning point of the discourse Jesus teaches on correct standing before God (6:1-6 and 6:16-18). The swivel around which the discourse is shaped (E) stands alone. It features Jesus' teaching his disciples how to pray, and what to pray (6:9-13: the Lord's Prayer). Summarizing, the Sermon on the Mount can be read as a chiasm: A (5:1-2) + B (5:3-16) + C (5:17-20) + D (5:21 — 6:8) + E (the centerpiece of 6:9-13) + D^1 (6:14 — 7:11) + C^1 (7:12) + B^1 (7:13-27) + A^1 (7:28 — 8:1a).[5]

Matthew 5:1-2 and 7:28 — 8:1a form a literary frame for the passage. Seeing great crowds, Jesus ascends the mountain, sits with his disciples, and teaches them (5:1-2). The sermon follows (5:3 — 7:27). It closes as Jesus finishes his teaching, descends from the mountain, and great crowds follow (7:28 — 8:1a). The Sermon opens with nine beatitudes, affirming the eschatological blessedness granted to those who hear Jesus' promises and follow him, and two brief parables insisting on what disciples are: salt and light to the earth (5:3-16). The first four beatitudes bless attitudes toward God (vv. 3-6), the second four attitudes toward others (vv. 7-10). The series closes with a declaration of end-time blessedness for the suffering experiences of the believing community (vv. 11-12). Living the beatitudes should not generate an elite, but provide meaning and direction for all the earth: salt and light (vv. 13-16).

A parallel series of instructions and warnings to believers about "the road that leads to life" closes the Sermon (7:13-27). The theme of the "kingdom of heaven" lies at the

---

5. See Luz, *Matthew*, 1:172-74. Not all agree. See Senior, *Matthew*, 67-69.

center of these two parallel passages. It appears in 5:3–16 (vv. 3, 10) and in 7:13–27 (v. 21).

A message central to the First Gospel introduces (5:17–20) and exits (7:12) the main section of the sermon. In 5:17–20, Jesus opens his sermon by insisting that he is not abolishing the Law and the prophets but bringing them to perfection and exhorts his followers to live in a way that manifests this belief. In 7:12, the same message is repeated in the well-known "golden rule": "Do to others whatever you would have them do to you. This is the law and the prophets."[6]

In 5:17–20, Matthew presents a "history of salvation," already raised in Jesus' encounter with John the Baptist (3:13–17). In 5:17–20, Jesus speaks of a time "now" when the Law and the prophets must be lived, and a later time, when "heaven and earth pass away." That will be a time in the future when "all things have taken place" (v. 18). The characters in Matthew's story, including Jesus, must live the Law and the Prophets until "heaven and earth pass away." There will be a time "later," when the Law and the prophets will be fulfilled (v. 17). From that time on, a new ethic will determine the way people relate to one another: "Do to others as you would have them do to you" (7:12).

A link with Jesus' insistence that he has come to bring the Law to perfection is found in 5:21–48. In these so-called antitheses Jesus explicitly cites the Law that his audience "has heard" (see vv. 21, 27, 31, 33, 38, 43). But asks his audience to go further *on the authority of his word*: "But I say to you" (see vv. 22, 28, 32, 34, 39, 44). Jesus does not suggest that the Law should be abandoned but asks that the motivation for moral imperatives come from the heart of the believer.

---

6. On the widespread use of "the golden rule," see Eduard Schweizer, *The Good News according to Matthew*, trans. David Green (London: SPCK, 1976), 174–75.

Jesus' Ministry of Preaching and Healing

Believers are to "go the extra mile" (see 5:41) because love lies at the heart of a Christian obedience to the Law.

This is made especially clear in the final antithesis (5:43-48). Loving those who love you is to live as nonbelievers. "Love your enemies, and pray for those who persecute you, that you may be children of your heavenly Father" (v. 44-45). Such a lifestyle *perfects* the Law (v. 17) and responds to Jesus' call that believers be *perfect* just as their heavenly Father is *perfect*.[7]

Paralleling Jesus' call to a deeper sensitivity to the demands of the Law, on the other side of the chiasm, he instructs his disciples on issues associated with right living: possessions, judging others, and the need to depend on God rather than oneself (6:19—7:11). They reflect "the three most important demonstrations of religious devotion in Judaism."[8] These two sections of the discourse, although different in literary form, are almost identical in length. They deal with the Christian approach to the Law of Israel that is not destroyed but lived from the heart: "For where your treasure is, there also will your heart be" (6:21). They form the bulk of Jesus' ethical teaching in the New Testament. The believer must always recognize that she or he ultimately stands before a judging God and Father (6:1-6; 6:16-18). "Your Father sees what is hidden and will repay you" (6:18; see vv. 4, 6, 8). Framing his teaching *what* to say in prayer (6:9-13), Jesus instructs his followers on *how* to pray: not babbling like the pagans (6:7-8), but with hearts full of forgiveness (6:14-15).

Jesus' prayer forms the heart of the discourse (6:9-13). The Sermon on the Mount demands a dependence on God, the Father of Jesus. Believers are to love and honor God as

---

7. In v. 17, Matthew uses the Greek verb *plēroō*, which means "fulfill." The adjective in v. 48 is *teleios*, meaning "perfect."
8. Schweizer, *Matthew*, 139.

their heavenly Father, ask that God's reigning presence in heaven be replicated on earth (vv. 9–10), and that God care for their daily needs (v. 11). Disciples must ask that the measure of God's forgiveness parallel their forgiveness of others (v. 12). As believers wait for the final coming of God in judgment, they beseech the God and Father of Jesus Christ to care for them. Loving response to the God who cares for the disciple, and the subsequent care that the disciples have for others, will be the measure of their judgment when it comes to the final test (see 25:31–54).[9]

MATTHEW 8:1B – 9:38: MIRACLES AND DISCIPLESHIP

Jesus' proclamation of the Gospel of the kingdom (see 8:23; 9:35) has been portrayed across the Sermon on the Mount. Matthew now turns to a systematic presentation of his "curing every disease and illness" (see 8:23; 9:35). Although almost all the miracles appear in the Gospel of Mark, Matthew pares them back to their essentials. "Matthew's account of Jesus' healing is so pruned of all auxiliary narrative details that the focus falls on the person's confidence in the power of Jesus."[10] The theme of discipleship, first broached in 4:18-22, is closely associated with the nine miracles in 8:1b – 11:1.

Matthew regularly shapes his narrative as triads, that is, in sets of three. He reports three sets of three miracles (8:1-17; 8:23 – 9:8; 9:18-34). Between the miracles Jesus teaches

---

9. The Greek word *peirasmos* means both the "temptations" of daily life and a time of "trial." The prayer does not ask God to desist from leading us into the temptations of daily life, but that we respond to God's gifts, and consequently be safe when the end-time trial comes (see Matt 25:31-46).

10. Garland, *Reading Matthew*, 91.

the radical nature of discipleship (8:18–22), calls the disciple Matthew from his tax office (9:9–13), and asks the disciples to pray to the Lord to send laborers into the burgeoning harvest (9:35–38). The need for laborers to reach out in mission leads to Jesus' institution of the Twelve, followed by a discourse instructing them on the challenges and blessings of that mission (10:1 – 11:1). For Matthew, writing in the late 80s of the first century, Jesus' discourse addresses the issues that will always face Christian missionaries.

The Shape of Matthew 8:1b—9:38: Nine Miracles and Discipleship

Three miracles (8:1b-17) and discipleship (vv. 18-22)
Three miracles (8:23—9:8) and discipleship (9:9-17)
Three miracles (9:18-34) and discipleship (vv. 35-38)

THE FIRST CYCLE OF MIRACLES AND THE DEMANDS OF DISCIPLESHIP *(8:1B–22)*

The cleansing of a leper opens the series (8:1b-4; see Mark 1:40-45). Matthew reports the request for a cure and Jesus' positive response. Jesus cures the leper with his word (v. 3). Nevertheless, he must show himself to the priest and offer the required gift for proof of his cure to fulfill the requirements of the Law (v. 4; see Lev 14:2-9). Jesus has restored a social and religious outcast to God's people. Jesus heals a centurion's son (vv. 5-13; see Luke 7:1-10). Overwhelmed by the faith of a Gentile, in contrast to the little faith found in Israel, Jesus foretells a time when many will come from east and west to recline at the table of Israel's fathers, while "the children of the kingdom will be driven out" (vv. 10-12). Jesus' word heals the child, from a distance (v. 13).

The series closes with a further boundary-breaking encounter (see Mark 1:29–31). Jesus takes the hand of Peter's ailing mother-in-law, a countercultural action for a righteous Jew. She is cured and she serves food to the group, again something unexpected (vv. 14–15). The first cycle closes with a summary of Jesus' miraculous activity, stressing his powerful word (v. 16), and an indication that his actions fulfill the prophecy of Isaiah: "He took away our infirmities and bore our diseases" (v. 17; see Isa 53:4).

The authority of Jesus reaches beyond the cultural and religious boundaries of Israel. At the center of the cycle, Jesus points forward to the future presence of the Gentiles among God's people (8:10–12). Nevertheless, the Law and the Scriptures must be fulfilled (vv. 4, 17).

Two potential disciples present themselves to Jesus (vv. 18–22). A scribe indicates his willingness to follow Jesus wherever he may go (v. 19), and a current disciple asks to be excused from his "following" so that he might bury his father (v. 21). Matthew uses these two characters to instruct all would-be disciples on the radical—and even harsh—nature of the call. They are following someone who has no resting place (v. 20); not even the closest of family ties can be allowed to interfere with adherence to Jesus (v. 22).

The Second Cycle of Miracles, he Call of Matthew to Discipleship, and the Preservation of the Old and the New (8:23 – 9:17)

Three spectacular miracles follow (vv. 23–27, 28–34; 9:1–8). In a boat, struck by a sudden storm at sea, literally an "earthquake," disciples who follow him lose hope, and call on Jesus to save them (vv. 23–25). Jesus describes them

Jesus' Ministry of Preaching and Healing

as "you of little faith" (v. 26: *oligopistoi*). Disciples who follow, the symbol of the boat as the Church, and the threat of destruction by an earthquake, point the audience beyond events that happened on the lake. For Matthew, this relationship to Jesus marks several of Matthew's portrayal of the disciples (see also 6:30; 14:31; 16:8). They believe, but they do not believe enough (see 6:30; 14:31; 16:8). Matthew's story invites Jesus' followers into unconditional faith in what God has done in and through Jesus. The violence threatening the community is reduced to a great calm by Jesus' word of rebuke, and the disciples wonder "what kind of man is this?" (vv. 26–27). Only God is master of the sea (see Job 38:8–11; Pss 29:3–4; 65:5–7; 89:8–10; 93:4; 106:9; 107:23–32). Despite the miracle, they are still wondering (v. 27).

The central miracle in the second cycle of three also reaches beyond the borders of Israel. Two demoniacs come from tombs in the region of the Gadarenes, on the far side of the sea (v. 28). More aware of Jesus' identity than the disciples in the storm (see v. 27), they address Jesus as "Son of God," questioning why he is coming to torment them before the appointed end-time (v. 29). A herd of swine is grazing in this Gentile land. At the demoniacs' request, the demons possess the swine that rush down the cliff into the sea and perish (vv. 30–32). Jesus has cleansed an impure Gentile region; two Gentiles have been cleansed of their demon possession. This new force for good, the presence of the Son of God, is not wanted. The townsfolk ask Jesus to leave the region (vv. 33–34).

Jesus returns to Israel, to "his own town." He forgives the sins of a paralytic (vv. 1–2). Scribes do not accept the authority of Jesus, and accuse him of blasphemy for forgiving sin, an authority only granted to God. He reduces them to silence and the crowd to the praise of God by demonstrating his authority over sickness and sin as the Son of Man. The crowd recognizes that God is giving such authority to humans (v. 8). For the first time in Jesus' public ministry the Scribes, members of Israel's leadership, question him (v. 3).

The second set of three miracles is followed by the account of the call of Matthew and its consequences (9:9-13; see Mark 2:13-17). A brief narrative repeats the literary paradigm for the call of the disciples in 3:18-22. Jesus is passing by, he summons Matthew from his customs post, and he "follows" him wordlessly (9:9). Resistance comes, once more from Israel's leadership. The Pharisees object to Jesus' company: tax collectors and sinners (vv. 10-11). In the miracles to this point Jesus has touched a leper (8:3), healed a Gentile (8:13), visited a Gentile land with its pigs and demons. Shortly, he will be touched by a woman with a flow of blood, and he will take the hand of a dead girl (9:25). He is not establishing an elite; he offers discipleship to those who need healing. His ministry, and that of his followers, seeks mercy, not sacrifice (vv. 12-13).

Disciples of John ask why the Pharisees and John's disciples fast, but Jesus' company does not (v. 14). Jesus points out that something new is among them in the person of the bridegroom. There is no call for fasting for the forgiveness of sins. Jesus has dispensed such forgiveness (see vv. 9-13). But suffering looms: "The days will come when the bridegroom is taken away from them." That will be the time for his disciples to fast (v. 15). Matthew rewrites Mark 2:18-22 to insist upon the continuity and value of all that comes from Israel's sacred history, and the newness that Jesus brings. For Mark, "the old" passes away, and the newness must be grasped (see Mark 2:22). For Matthew, the old and the new must be preserved. "The old" retains its ongoing significance as Israel and its sacred history does not end in Jesus; it is brought to its perfection (see Matt 5:17). The audi-

Jesus' Ministry of Preaching and Healing

ence will eventually discover that Jesus' death and resurrection, when Jesus is "taken away" from them, will mark "the turning point of the ages."[11]

THE THIRD CYCLE OF MIRACLES AND JESUS' REQUEST FOR LABORERS TO WORK IN THE ABUNDANT HARVEST (9:18–38)

The miracles of the official's daughter (9:18–19, 23–26) and the woman with the flow of blood (vv. 20–22; see Mark 5:21–43) form a single miracle embedded in a so-called sandwich construction, a form of intercalation. The faith of the official (Matt 9:18) leads Jesus to take his daughter by the hand and restore her to life (v. 25). The faith of the woman leads her to touch Jesus, and she is cured. As with the cure of Peter's mother-in-law (see 8:14–15), a procession of "touches" restores two women. As a result of her touching Jesus (vv. 20–21), the woman with the flow of blood is no longer excluded from Israel's life and cult. Jesus takes the hand of the young girl and she is no longer excluded from life itself. Jesus' fame "spread throughout all that land" (v. 26).

The healing of the two blind men follows. It is loosely based on Mark's account of the healing of the blind Bartimaeus (Mark 10:46–52) but appears much earlier in the First Gospel. They appeal to Jesus as "Son of David," reinforcing Matthew's portrait of Jesus as the Davidic shepherd messiah (Matt 8:27). Inside the house he interrogates them on their recognition of Jesus' authority, he touches them, and they regain their sight (28–30a). Sworn to secrecy,

---

11. The expression comes from John Meier. See John P. Meier, *Matthew*, New Testament Message 3 (Wilmington, DE: Michael Glazier, 1980), xi–xii, 46–47.

they ignore Jesus' instruction and "spread word of him through all that land" (vv. 30b–31; see v. 26).

The growing fame of Jesus leads to a further miracle and rejection from the leaders of Israel in verses 32–34 (see Luke 11:14–15). Jesus drives out a demon that rendered a man mute, and the man speaks (vv. 11–12a). The crowds manifest amazement, stating that "nothing like this has ever been seen in Israel" (v. 33).[12] But the leaders of Israel have a different assessment of Jesus' miraculous activity, a cycle of which is now coming to its end. For them, "He drives out demons by the prince of demons" (v. 34). They disassociate Jesus from the gifts of God and associate him with the powers of evil. On the one hand, tension between Jesus and Israel's leadership is growing, while these three miracles are the fruit of a turning to Jesus in faith.

Matthew's careful plotting of Jesus' teaching and healing closes as it began: "Jesus went around to all the towns and villages, teaching in their synagogues, proclaiming the Gospel of the kingdom, and curing every disease and illness" (9:35; see 4:23). The sheep of Jesus' flock are without a shepherd (v. 36; see Mark 6:34). The compassion shown across the miracle stories continues. The Davidic shepherd messiah cannot endure the people's lack of direction. He summons his disciples, points to the abundant harvest before them, lamenting the scarcity of laborers for the harvest. They are to ask God, Jesus' father, the master of the harvest, to send out laborers (v. 37–38). Jesus' final instruction of his disciples across the nine miracles that shape 8:1b – 9:38 points the narrative further. He chooses the Twelve (10:1–4), commissions them for service (vv. 5–15), and instructs

---

12. The "crowds" appear regularly in the First Gospel. They are neither "for" or "against" Jesus. Their favor can swing either way. See Davies and Allison, *Saint Matthew*, 1:419–20.

them on their mission among the sheep without a shepherd (10:6—11:1).

MATTHEW 10:1—11:1: THE TWELVE AND THE MISSIONARY DISCOURSE

Having invited disciples to ask the master for laborers for his harvest (9:38), Jesus chooses twelve of them for a specific ministry. Matthew opens and closes the discourse on mission with reference to "the Twelve" (10:1; 11:1).

The Shape of Matthew 10:1—11:1:
The Sermon on Mission

Frame: Jesus institutes the Twelve (10:1-4)
    A Jesus sends out the Twelve to repeat his mission
        (vv. 5-15)
        B Jesus encourages them to face future suffering
            (vv. 16-23)
            C They will share the fate of their master (vv. 24-25)
Centerpiece: "Have no fear" (vv. 26-31)
            C^1 Jesus will speak for them in the day of reckoning
                (vv. 32-33)
        B^1 Invitation to take up the cross and be receptive in the
            face of suffering (vv. 34-39)
    A^1 As Jesus is sent, so are they (vv. 40-42)
Frame: Jesus completes his instruction of the Twelve (11:1)

Until this point in the story, only Jesus has overcome evil spirits and cured disease, illness, and even death. The Twelve are "given authority" to do the same (10:1). Matthew names them "apostles," meaning "those sent." At this stage of the story, he does not instruct them "to teach" as he has taught in 5:1—8:1a. That aspect of their ministry must wait until Jesus has been crucified and risen. Part of the "turning point of the ages," they will be authorized to teach as he taught (see 28:19-20).

Matthew provides their names (vv. 2-4). This is the only time he uses the expression "apostle" for the Twelve, but it leads into his use of the associated verb *apostellō* to open and close the description of their "sending" (vv. 5 and 16). In verses 40-42, it closes Jesus' description of the negative and positive fruits of the mission (vv. 17-42). Jesus limits the ministry of the Twelve to the lost sheep of Israel (vv. 5-6). Like John the Baptist (3:2) and Jesus (4:17), the missionaries proclaim the pressing nearness of God's reigning presence as king in the lives and hearts of all: "The kingdom of heaven is at hand" (v. 7); but only to Israel.

This puzzling limitation will characterize the mission of Jesus and the Twelve throughout the Gospel. Jesus is rarely present in a Gentile land. He has purified Gadara of its uncleanliness (9:28-34) but the townsfolk asked him to leave (v. 34). Jesus "withdraws" to the region of Tyre and Sidon in 15:21. On that occasion, the Canaanite woman "comes out," crossing into Israel, asking him to cure her daughter. He applies to himself his instruction to the Twelve in 10:5-6: "I was sent only to the lost sheep of Israel" (15:24). For Matthew, Jesus brings to perfection the Law and the prophets (5:17) in his fulfillment of Israel's Scriptures, within the geographical limits of Israel. As he earlier instructed John the Baptist, who refused to baptize him: "Allow it for now" (3:15).

There will be a time "later" when this will change. "Until heaven and earth pass away, not the smallest letter or the smallest part of a letter will pass from the law, until all things have taken place" (5:18). The use of the expres-

Jesus' Ministry of Preaching and Healing

sion "until" (*heōs*) indicates a later time. There is a narrative "time" between the situation of Jesus and the disciples "now," and a "not yet" that lies in the future. Then, as the audience will eventually discover, all national and religious boundaries will disappear (28:16–20).

The discourse can be read as a chiasm.[13] It instructs disciples on mission that they should have no fear in the face of suffering and rejection.

> A. *Vv. 5–15.* Jesus sends the Twelve on mission. They repeat the ministry of Jesus (vv. 7–8), associating themselves with his lifestyle as a wandering charismatic who depends on God (vv. 9–10). Adopting a sign used by Israelites to indicate that they are in unholy land, they are to bring peace to homes and towns, but shake off the dust from their feet as a sign of judgment and their eventual destruction when their words are not heard (vv. 12–15).
> B. *Vv. 16–23.* They are encouraged to suffer the consequences of their mission. Jesus spells out details that reflect the conditions and experiences of the mission of the earliest Christians, trials, and family betrayals.
>> C. *Vv. 24–25.* They are to share the fate of their Master.
>>> D. *Vv. 26–31.* At the center of the discourse they are told, "Have no fear" (v. 26). Called to courage in a setting of rejection and persecution (vv. 26–33), the Twelve (and through them Matthew's audience) are to have no fear. God is their Father who cares for them in all times and circumstances (vv. 29–31).

---

13. See Davies and Allison, *Saint Matthew*, 2.162.

THE SHAPE OF MATTHEW'S STORY

C^1. *Vv. 32-33.* As they follow Jesus in their experience of persecution, Jesus is the one who will speak for (or against) them before the Father on the day of reckoning (vv. 32-33).

B^1. *Vv. 34-39.* Divided families, the very basic structure of society, will result from the divisive power of Jesus' word (vv. 34-39). Jesus spells out the fundamental conditions of discipleship: cross and receptivity. Jesus must be loved above all else and everyone else (v. 37). A disciple unwilling to take up a cross is not worthy of their master. Loss of life for the sake of Jesus is to gain life (vv. 38-39).

A^1. *Vv. 40-42.* As Jesus was sent, so are they. The believer *receives* Jesus and his word, prophets bearing that word, the righteous who live that word, and Jesus' fragile disciples ("these little ones"), who seek that word. Openness to Jesus and receptivity to his word within a community of believers will be rewarded (vv. 40-42).

The story of Jesus' ministry of preaching and healing, discipleship, community, and mission (4:17—11:1) ends with a formula that parallels the close of the sermon on the mount: "When Jesus finished giving these commands to his twelve disciples, he went away from that place to teach and to preach in their towns" (11:1; see 7:28—8:1a). Miracles took place in "his own town" (9:1). He now moves away "from that place" (11:1).

> Matthew's storytelling techniques guide the audience through the narrative of 4:17—11:1. His use of summary statements about Jesus' preaching and healing in 4:23 and 9:35 frame his preaching (5:1—8:1a) and healing (8:1b—9:34). He shapes 5:1—8:1a as a chiasm. His threefold cyclic

Jesus' Ministry of Preaching and Healing

use of three miracles, in which each cycle is followed by Gospel teaching on the call to discipleship and its challenges (8:18-22; 9:9-17; 9:35-38), has led directly into the call and commissioning of the Twelve, and the discourse on mission, another chiasm (10:1—11:1). Jesus' ministry, limited to Israel, fulfills the Scriptures (8:17; see Isa 53:4). Hints emerge that there will be a later time when the Law and the prophets will be perfected (8:10-12; 10:5-6).

CHAPTER FOUR

The Crisis in the Ministry of the Messiah
Matthew 11:2 – 16:23

The shape of Matthew's story becomes harder to trace. Some suggest that he begins to display "editorial fatigue."[1] Nevertheless, three major themes emerge: the person of Jesus, his rejection by the leaders of Israel, and the foundation of his "new family." The passage unfolds in two sections.

    1. Matthew 11:2–14:12 opens with the question of John the Baptist, leading to discussion of the roles of Jesus and John (11:2-19). It closes with the account of the execution of John the Baptist (14:1-12).

    2. Two bread miracles (14:13-21; 15:32-39) determine the shape of 14:13–16:23. Israel's leadership rejects Jesus' authority and the disciples show that they are "of little faith."

    An inclusion between the Baptist's poignant question about Jesus' messianic identity (11:2-14) and Peter's response to that question in his confession of Jesus as the Son of Man, the Christ, and the Son of the living God (16:13-20) determines the outside limits of 11:2–16:23. The first

---

1. See Davies and Allison, *Saint Matthew*, 1:71-72.

passion prediction and Peter's response (16:21-23) brings his confession to hesitant closure, opening the way for Jesus' journey to Jerusalem (16:13—20:34). Matthew 16:13-23 serves as a "bridge episode," looking back across the narrative to this point (vv. 13-20) and opening the door to what is yet to come (vv. 21-23). It plays a role in the narrative strategies of *both* 14:13—16:23 (which it closes) and 16:13—20:34 (which it opens).

Between the inclusion of 11:2-19 and 14:1-12, the audience encounters intercalations of four rejections of Jesus and his disciples (11:20-24; 12:1-14, 22-37, 43-45) and four affirmations of Jesus and his new family (11:25-30; 12:15-21, 38-42, 46-50). The parable discourse (13:1-58) condemns Israel's leaders and blesses the disciples. These themes develop around Jesus' feeding Israel (14:13-21), and a wider audience (15:32-39). In the aftermath of each feeding miracle, the disciples struggle to accept Jesus unconditionally (14:22-33; 16:1-12), despite his spectacular works (14:22-34; 15:21-31). Israel continues to resist (15:1-20), while a Gentile and Galileans show great faith (15:21-31).

MATTHEW 11:1—14:12: ARE YOU THE ONE WHO IS TO COME?

This poignant question from the imprisoned John the Baptist (11:3) hangs over the narrative. The alternation between rejection and affirmation of Jesus and his role across 11:20—13:58 shows two possible responses to John's question. This literary "back and forth" indicates a crisis that calls the audience to decision.

THE SHAPE OF MATTHEW'S STORY

**The Shape of Matthew 11:2—14:12:
Are You the One Who Is to Come?**

Frame: Jesus and John the Baptist (11:2-19)
   Rejection: Unrepentant towns (11:20-24)
      Affirmation: The Father and the Son (11:25-30)
   Rejection: Sabbath conflicts between Israel's leaders and
      the Son of Man (12:1-14)
   Affirmation: The chosen Servant (12:15-21)
   Rejection: Jesus and Beelzebul (12:22-37)
      Affirmation: Jesus and the sign of Jonah (12:38-42)
   Rejection: Return of the unclean spirit (12:43-45)
      Affirmation: The criterion for the new family of Jesus
      (12:46-50)
   Exclusion and inclusion: The parable discourse (13:1-53)
   Rejection: Rejection at Nazareth (13:54-58)
Frame: Jesus and John the Baptist (14:1-12)

OPENING FRAME: JOHN THE BAPTIST (11:2-19)

John asks from prison, having heard of "the deeds of the Messiah" (*ta erga tou Christou*), whether Jesus is that expected Messiah (11:2-3). Jesus points to the "deeds" (*erga*) of chapters 8—9 that fulfill the messianic expectation of Isaiah (vv. 4-6; see Isa 19:18-19; 35:5-6). His "words" of chapters 5—7 also point to the identity of Jesus: "and the poor have the good news proclaimed to them" (v. 5). Jesus utters an ominous beatitude: "Blessed is the one who takes no offence at me" (v. 6). The possibility of rejection or acceptance emerges.

Jesus both praises and subordinates the Baptist. John is a prophet, and more than a prophet: he is the forerunner of the Christ (vv. 7-10, 14-15). He is the greatest figure from the past, marking the end of the Law and the Prophets (see 5:17-20). His era marks the turning point between the time before and after the advent of the kingdom of heaven where all who enter that kingdom will enjoy a greatness even superior to John (vv. 11-12). But the violence soon to be suffered by John (see 14:1-12) will also be experienced by Jesus. Violence and rejection mark the clash between God and the powers of evil in the establishment of the kingdom (v. 12). Jesus draws a comparison between John the Baptist, now in prison, and the Son of Man. "This generation," the leaders of Israel, are like children playing in the marketplace unable to accept the contrasting roles of the ascetic John and the more accessible Jesus (vv. 16-19a). Wisdom, the divine plan for humankind, is vindicated "by her deeds" (v. 19b: *tōn ergon autēs*; see v. 2: *ta erga tou Christou*).

Rejection (11:20-24)

Jesus condemns three towns in Galilee: Chorazin, Bethsaida, and Capernaum. They have rejected "most of his mighty deeds" (v. 20). They "will go down into the netherworld" (v. 23). The Gentile towns of Tyre and Sidon would have repented. The proverbially corrupt Sodom (see Gen 18-19) would have been saved if it had been offered the same opportunities (vv. 23-24).

Affirmation (11:25-30)

Jesus praises God as "Father," claiming that certain truths have been made known to the childlike because of the intimate relationship of knowledge that exists between the Father (God) and the Son (Jesus), and the Son's desire to make them known. These words reflect the mysterious presence of the divine in Jesus. His claim of a father-son relationship with God does not separate him from the people, to whom he has spoken (5:1 – 7:29) and whose infirmities he has healed (8:1 – 9:34). They represent those who recognize their needs, and not those whose wisdom and learning lead to arrogance. Israel accepts the life-giving "yoke" of the Law. Jesus offers a yoke of his own, marked by his compassion (see 9:35-38). He desires mercy, not sacrifice (see 12:7), and depends on his intimacy with God, his Father (12:25-27). The disciples are to "learn (*mathete*)" from Jesus.

Rejection (12:1–14)

The Pharisees complain to Jesus about his disciples picking grain on a Sabbath. He recalls an episode from Israel's sacred history (see 1 Sam 21:2-7), and the instruction of the Law on the legitimate behavior of the priests in the temple on a Sabbath (Lev 24:5-9; Num 28:9-10). This conflict is resolved by recourse to the word of God, and a christological claim that "something greater than the temple is here" (v. 6). On the same Sabbath Jesus meets a man with a withered hand in their synagogue. The Pharisees question whether he should cure on a Sabbath (vv. 9-10). Jesus insists on the need to do good for a human being on a Sabbath (vv. 11-12). The second conflict is resolved by the authority of Jesus' word: "Stretch out your hand" (v. 13). The Pharisees decide that Jesus must be put to death (v. 14).

Despite rejection, Jesus emerges from these conflicts as one who behaves according to Israel's traditions (vv. 3-5). Indeed, he chastises the Pharisees for not being aware of these traditions: "have you not read?" (vv. 3, 5). The Son of Man is the lord of the Sabbath (v. 8). Jesus does not violate the Sabbath; he shows that he and his disciples are without guilt in these controversies. Matthew's positive portrait of Jesus develops in these conflictual situations that will lead to death (v. 14).

The Crisis in the Ministry of the Messiah

Affirmation (12:15-21)

To this point in his story, Matthew has told of a compassionate Jesus (8:17; 9:35-38; 11:4-5, 28-30; 12:7, 12). It has led Pharisees to decide that he must be executed (12:14). Matthew reports that Jesus "withdrew from that place" (v. 15). In an unknown location he works further cures for an unknown crowd, commands to silence (vv. 15-16), and is identified as the fulfillment of Isaiah's Suffering Servant (vv. 18-21; see Isa 42:1-4). In a setting marked by the promise of violence (v. 14), Jesus the Servant brings love, the Spirit, gentleness, and justice to God's chosen people. His "withdrawal" (v. 15) promises his future proclamation of justice to the Gentiles (v. 18); his name will bring hope to the Gentiles (v. 21).

Rejection (12:22-37)

Faced with the crowd's possible recognition of Jesus as the Son of David, resulting from his cure of a deaf mute (vv. 22-23), the Pharisees indicate their assessment of Jesus' power over sickness and evil: "This man drives out demons only by the power of Beelzebul, the prince of demons" (v. 24). Jesus addresses the issue of the source of goodness and forgiveness (vv. 25-37). Satan cannot drive out Satan as such action would divide the satanic kingdom. By whose authority do Israel's miracle workers do good and not evil: God or the prince of demons? Jesus drives out demons by the Spirit of God; the kingdom and its accompanying power have arrived (vv. 26-29).

The Pharisees are making a fundamental error as they claim that the Spirit of God is the presence of the "prince of demons." They exclude themselves from forgiveness in this age and the age to come. All sins can be forgiven, but a denial of the presence of the Spirit of God and the kingdom of God renders the source of all forgiveness unavailable (vv. 30–32). The Pharisees had accused Jesus of blasphemy in 9:3. Matthew's story of Jesus presents them as committing a greater blasphemy.

The experience of fruit from a good or rotten tree exemplifies Jesus' teaching. Good comes from good, and vice versa (vv. 33 and 35). The Pharisees have shown themselves rotten. They are a brood of vipers who can only manifest the evil that is in their hearts (v. 34). To state that Jesus' goodness is driven by the prince of demons is to utter a fundamentally evil word, leading to judgment and condemnation (vv. 36–37).

Affirmation (12:38–42)

Jesus refuses to provide the scribes and the Pharisees with a sign that validates the authority of his healing presence and his teaching (v. 38). He promises this "evil and unfaithful generation" that they will be offered only the sign of Jonah. Will Israel be converted by the Son of Man's being "in the heart of the earth three days and three nights" (vv. 39–40)? Matthew's community, facing hostility from the synagogue across the road toward the end of the first Christian century, is aware that it did not happen (see 27:62–66; 28:11–15). Jonah's preaching converted sinful Nineveh. The Queen of the South came to hear the wisdom of Solomon. She will rise in condemnation of this unbelieving generation. As hostility increases, Matthew has foretold the resurrection of Jesus and affirmed that his greatness exceeds that of Jonah and the Queen of the South. Jesus, the wisdom of God, the sign of Jonah, is rejected by the leaders of Israel.

Rejection (12:43–45)

The experience of a late-first-century Christian community continues in Jesus' incisive remarks about an unclean spirit that once possessed a person but went out, searching for rest in other regions (v. 43). For Matthew's view of God's saving history, this moment reflects Jesus' victory over Satan: "Then the devil left him" (4:11). On return, the devil finds the household "empty, swept clean, and put in order" (12:44). Such Satan-free orderliness is the result of Jesus' presence in Israel (see 5:17-20). However, Israel rejected and executed Jesus. Accompanied by seven more evil spirits, the devil returns to faithless Israel, and leaves it in a condition "worse than the first." This is Matthew's judgment on "this evil generation," a hostile Israel that rejected Jesus and continues to reject his followers (v. 45).

Affirmation (12:46-50)

Jesus has gathered disciples and instructed them (4:18-22; 8:18-22; 9:9-13; 9:35-38; 10:1-15). The blood family of Jesus, his mother and his brothers are "outside" wishing to speak to him. He hears this news while speaking to the crowds (vv. 46, 48). Jesus does not criticize his blood family; he points to the greater possibilities and dignity of his "faith-family" as he singles out his disciples. A new criterion emerges for the *universal possibility* of belonging to the family of Jesus: "*whoever* (*hostis*) does the will of my heavenly Father is my brother, and sister, and mother" (vv. 49-50).

EXCLUSION AND INCLUSION: THE PARABLE DISCOURSE *(13:1-53)*

Matthew's rhythmic balance of rejections and affirmations of Jesus pauses. Jesus tells seven parables and reflects on the use of parables. The discourse intensifies the growing distance between Jesus and Israel, and the increasing importance of the disciples. After an introduction (13:1-3a),

THE SHAPE OF MATTHEW'S STORY

Matthew again has recourse to triads as he shapes the parable discourse into three moments, determined by parables, reflection on their use, and their interpretation.[2]

> The Parable of the Sower (vv. 3b–9)
>   "Why do you speak to them in parables?" (v. 10),
>   with reference to the Scriptures (vv. 10–17)
>   Interpretation of the parable of the sower
>   (vv. 18–23)
> Three parables: weeds, mustard seed, and yeast
>   (vv. 24–33)
>   Reflection on the use of parables, with reference to
>   the Scriptures (vv. 34–35)
>   "Explain to us the parable" (v. 36): interpretation of
>   the parable of the weeds (vv. 36–43)
> Three parables: hidden treasure, pearl, and net
>   (vv. 44–48)
>   Interpretation of the parable of the net (vv. 49–50)
>   Conclusion: "Do you understand all these things?"
>   (v. 51): treasures both new and old (vv. 51–53)

Jesus leaves the crowd by the sea and addresses them from a boat (vv. 1–3a), symbolizing his movement away from Israel, and his association with the disciples. The parable of the sower (vv. 3b–9) is a statement of the mixed reception that Jesus' teaching has received. Not all the seed prospers. The parable closes with a summons that is also a warning: "Whoever has ears ought to hear" (v. 9). In response to the disciples' question about his use of parables (v. 10), Jesus draws a line between those who have been granted knowledge of the mysterious ways of the kingdom of heaven, and those who have not. The former will prosper in that kingdom; the latter will lose even what they have. They will be punished (v. 12), fulfilling the prophecy of Isaiah 6:9–10,

---

2. See Davies and Allison, *Saint Matthew*, 2:370–72.

refusing to hear or see because they have no desire to be converted (vv. 14–15). On the other hand, the disciples are privileged because they are gifted with hearing and seeing, unlike earlier generations of prophets and righteous people (vv. 16–17).

In the interpretation of the parable (vv. 18–23), Matthew warns disciples. Jesus has indicated the privileged status of those who hear and see, but there can be no complacency. Even the most enthusiastic outward response to the Gospel offers no guarantee that one is a true disciple. Lack of understanding of Jesus' word (v. 19), its superficial reception (vv. 20–21), and the troubles and anxieties of this world (vv. 22) can lead to fruitlessness. Only rich soil, true hearing, and understanding bears much fruit (v. 23). The disciples might be "privileged" (v. 11), but they are challenged to persevere in their fruitful reception of the word of Jesus (vv. 18–23).

In rapid succession, Jesus tells parables of weeds sown among the wheat by an evil man (vv. 24–30: only in the First Gospel), the mustard seed (vv. 31–32) and the yeast (v. 33), from Mark (4:30–32) and from Q (Luke 13:20–21), respectively. The first parable sets the theme. The wheat and the weeds must grow together. The "field" for this mixed crop can be the world, or even the community. As conflict and opposition are a reality for Jesus (11:2 — 12:50), so will they be for his followers. Believers must be prepared to live, thrive, and persevere, despite the existence of evil in the world, and in the community. At the harvest, reapers will gather the weeds for destruction and the wheat that will be stored in the master's barn. The master is the judge (v. 30).

In the light of this ambiguity, the two parables describe inevitable growth: the smallest seed becomes the greatest of shrubs (vv. 31–32) and the yeast in three measures of flour produces enough bread to feed a large crowd of people

(v. 33). These processes, once set in motion, are unstoppable. No matter how challenging hostile opposition might be, the kingdom's growth is inevitable.

Repeating the literary pattern of the first trio of episodes, Jesus explains "to the crowds" why he addresses them only in parables: they hear "what has been hidden from the foundation of the world." There is no explicit rejection of those who do not hear and understand, as in verses 10–17, but Jesus focuses on the crowds as those whose reception of his parables fulfills Psalm 78:2. He has opened his mouth in parables, announcing what has lain hidden. But the leaders of Israel have not listened.

Jesus dismisses the crowds and enters "the house" (v. 36). The mysteries of the kingdom have been hidden from Israel (v. 11). The disciples ask for an explanation of the parable of the weeds. He responds in verses 36–53. The good seed, sown by the Son of Man, are the children of the kingdom, while the weeds are the children of the evil one, sown by the devil. The eschatological reapers are angels, and the Son of Man acts as the final judge of good and evil. The righteous are promised a glorious future "in the kingdom of their father" (v. 42a). Their victory is inevitable (see vv. 31–33), but everyone must face eschatological judgment.

The final trio of parables (13:44–50) initially describes the inestimable worth of the kingdom of heaven: a treasure in a field (v. 44) and a pearl of great worth (vv. 45–46). The kingdom is beyond all price, and one must be wholeheartedly committed to possess it. The final parable, the separation of the good from the bad fish (vv. 47–48), enables Matthew to return to his insistence on the end of time, explaining the parable of the wheat and the weeds (see vv. 39–43). The evil ones will be cast into the fire where there will be weeping and grinding of teeth (vv. 47–50). Evil will not last forever; God will prevail (see 6:2-4; 8:12; 22:13; 24:51; 25:30).

This discourse closes with a firm commitment from the disciples that they have understood "all these things," the mysteries of the kingdom, unveiled in Jesus' parables (v. 51; see v. 11). It remains to be seen whether that is true or not. In the meantime, Jesus describes "every scribe who is trained for the kingdom" (v. 52), to instruct them what such understanding should generate. Widely regarded as a brief autobiographical pen-picture, the affirmation situates the storyteller and his audience in a Jewish scribal world ("every scribe") now "disciplined" for participation in the newness of the kingdom of heaven that arrived with Jesus (see 3:2; 4:17). The Greek for "disciplined" (*mathēteutheis*) is the verbal form of the word used to describe a disciple (*mathētēs*): one who learns.

The story of Jesus to this point shows that the action of God in his Son, revealed by his words and his actions, reshapes Israel's traditions. The old is reread in the light of the new. For Matthew, the Christian looks back to Israel's sacred tradition, and regards it as a treasure. Jesus has not abandoned that treasure but "fulfills" it (see 1:22; 2:5, 17, 23; 3:3; 4:14; 8:17; 12:15; 13:14, 34). The believer brings forth both old and new from his treasure. As Jesus said when describing the old and new wine and skins: "both are preserved" (9:17).

Matthew ends the discourse with his stereotypical: "When Jesus had finished these parables, he left that place" (13:53; see 7:28-29; 11:1; 19:1). Despite its being "an interlude," the parables of 13:1-53 continue the theme of rejection and affirmation from Jesus' perspective. The disciples are affirmed, but Israel's leaders are threatened with rejection (vv. 10-15).

THE SHAPE OF MATTHEW'S STORY

Rejection (13:54–58)

The final rejection takes place in Jesus' hometown (13:54–58). He teaches the people "in their synagogue" (v. 54). They ask the right question about the source of the authority he has manifested across 5:1 – 9:38 (vv. 54 and 56). Jesus proverbially points out that a prophet is not welcome in his own country (13:57–58). The disciples have shown "little faith" (*oligopistos* [6:30; 8:26]), but Jesus' townsfolk manifest "no faith" (13:58: *apistia*).

CLOSING FRAME: JOHN THE BAPTIST (14:1–12)

John the Baptist, the prophetic forerunner of the coming of the Lord (3:1–12), is also the prophetic forerunner of his death. Herod suspects that Jesus' powers indicate that he is John the Baptist risen from the dead (14:1–2; see also 16:14). Herod imprisoned John because, like Jesus, he fearlessly spoke out in favor of the Law (vv. 3–4; see 5:17–20). Like Jesus, the crowd regarded him as a prophet (v. 5; see 13:57; 27:17), although Jesus' role as a prophet has just been rejected in his own village (13:57). Like Pilate, the desire to please others leads Herod to execute John (vv. 5–11; see 27:11–26). Both prophets have been rejected (13:57; 14:5). Disciples bury John's body and inform Jesus (v. 12; see 27:57–61). The end of the forerunner's life matches the end of Jesus' life, with one exception. Despite Herod's suspicion that John had risen from the dead (v. 2), such is not the case. Jesus, not John the Baptist, rises from the dead (v. 12; 28:1–7).

The Crisis in the Ministry of the Messiah

MATTHEW 14:13 – 16:23: FEEDING AND FAILURE

Matthew shapes 14:13 – 16:23 around two feeding miracles and their aftermath. Against the increasing manifestation of Jesus' power and authoritative teaching, not only do the leaders of Israel fail, but Jesus' disciples do not understand him, manifesting "little faith."

The Shape of Matthew 14:13–16:23: Feeding and Failure

The first feeding miracle—in Israel (14:13-21)
Consequences: Israel, the disciples, and Peter fail. Jesus turns to the Gentiles (14:22—15:31)

1. Jesus comes to the disciples on the stormy sea. Peter shows "little faith" (14:22-33)
2. Jesus questions the traditions of Israel (15:1-14)
3. An ignorant Peter asks Jesus for a clarification of his teaching (15:15-20)
4. Healing of a Canaanite woman; healing and praise for the God of Israel in a Gentile land (15:21-31)

The second feeding miracle—among the Gentiles (15:32-39)
Consequences: Israel, the disciples, and Peter fail (16:1-23)

1. The Pharisees seek a sign (16:1-4)
2. Crossing the sea, disciples "of little faith" discuss Jesus' words on the leaven (16:5-12)
3. Peter confesses that Jesus is the Son of Man, the Son of God. He is blessed (16:13-20)

4. Peter refuses to accept Jesus' first prediction that Messiah must suffer, die, and rise. He is cursed (16:21-23)

THE FIRST FEEDING MIRACLE – IN ISRAEL (14:13-21)

The geographical context for the first feeding miracle is Israel: the location of Jesus' hometown (13:54-58) and the unnamed place of the celebration of Herod's birthday (14:1-12: Machaerus in Galilee?). Jesus uses a boat to withdraw to a desert place, but the crowds follow him "from their own towns" (v. 13). Continuing his care for the lost sheep of Israel (see 8:17; 10:6; 15:24), he refuses the disciples' request that the crowds be sent back to their towns, insisting that they feed them (vv. 15-16). Out of the disciples' poverty (five loaves and two fish) he feeds the multitude of five thousand men and many women and children (vv. 19-21).

Several details point to the miraculous feeding as a nourishment of Israel. The crowds are to sit down on the grass for a meal, to have their hunger satisfied, recalling Psalm 23:1-5: "There is nothing I lack….In green pastures he makes me lie down.…You set a table before me." Matthew's description of Jesus' actions with the loaves and the fish recalls Jesus' final meal with his disciples: "taking… looking up to heaven…said the blessing…and gave them" (see Matt 26:26-30). The fragments left over fill twelve baskets (v. 20). The Greek word for "fragments" (*klasmata*) was used in the earliest Church to refer to the eucharistic species, the number "twelve" recalls the tribes of Israel, and the "wicker baskets" (*kophinoi*) refers to a distinctively Jewish receptacle. For Matthew's Church, the feeding miracle promises that the table generated by Jesus' use of his disciples to nourish Israel remains open (vv. 16 and 19).

First Consequence: The "Little Faith" of Peter and the Disciples (14:22–33)

Jesus, the disciples, and the crowd separate as Jesus sends them off in a boat, dismisses the crowd, and goes to pray alone on the mountain (vv. 22–23). During the fourth watch of the night, in the midst of a storm, he comes to them, walking on the water, assuming authority over the sea (see Job 9:8; 38:16; Sir 24:5–6; Ps 77:19). Despite the bread miracle they have witnessed, they are terrified, think they are seeing a ghost, and have to be assured that it is indeed Jesus. He uses an expression from the Hebrew Scriptures associated with divine revelation: "Take courage, it is I" (vv. 24–27; see Exod 3:14; 33:19–23; Num 11:17; Judg 6:11–24; 1 Kgs 19:11). Peter puts Jesus' authoritative self-revelation to the test, by asking him to perform another miracle. Called to join Jesus on the stormy waters, Peter's faith falters. As he sinks he calls for help. There is a depth of ecclesial significance in this encounter (vv. 28–31: the boat, Peter, the challenge of the storm, Peter's hesitant response, the call for help). Jesus asks, "Why did you doubt?" He provides the response, describing Peter as of "little faith" (*oligopiste*) (v. 32). The storm over, the disciples confess that Jesus is the Son of God (vv. 32–33). Matthew's disciples believe, but they still have a long way to go. They can say the right words, but cannot put their lives where their words are.

Unconditional trust in the saving touch of Jesus on his landing at Gennasareth contrasts the limited faith of the disciples (vv. 34–36). The faith of the people in Gennasareth is also contrasts sharply with the critical rejection of Jesus by the leaders of Israel in the passage that follows.

THE SHAPE OF MATTHEW'S STORY

Second Consequence: Questioning the Traditions of Israel (15:1–14)

Israel's leadership, Pharisees and scribes from Jerusalem, question Jesus about his disciples' disregard of "the tradition of the elders" in their eating practices (15:1-2). Matthew abbreviates Mark 7:1–23, intensifying the hostility between Jesus and his opponents. Jesus directly contrasts the Pharisees and the scribes' attitude to "the commandments of God," using an example of their care for parents that "nullifies" the word of God for the sake of their tradition (vv. 3–6). He uses Isaiah 29:13 to describe them: hearts far from God, teaching human laws as doctrines (vv. 8–9). He teaches the crowds that external practices do not defile, but only what comes from inside a person (vv. 10–11). To the disciples' concern that Israel's leaders might be offended, he describes them as blind guides (vv. 12–14). Jesus attacks the teaching of the elders, not the teaching of Israel.

Third Consequence: Peter and the Disciples' Ignorance (15:15–20)

As Peter asks for further clarification, Jesus addresses all the disciples, astonished at their lack of understanding (v. 16). He returns to the imagery used to speak to the crowd. Insisting that external practices do not defile, he lists the practices that do (vv. 17-19). They come from the heart, unlike the Jewish food laws (v. 20).

Fourth Consequence: The Canaanite Woman. Healing and Praise for the God of Israel in a Gentile Land (15:21–31)

Jesus "withdrew" from Israel, entering the Gentile region of Tyre and Sidon (v. 21). This is a decisive strategy to

The Crisis in the Ministry of the Messiah

locate Jesus in a area outside Israel. The Canaanite woman, in radical contrast to the leaders of Israel, the crowd, Peter and the disciples (see vv. 1-20), accepts rejection by the disciples (v. 23b), by Jesus (v. 24), and an insult (v. 26). She persists in her request for the health of her daughter, based entirely on her faith in Jesus as "Lord, Son of David" (vv. 22, 25, 27). The second miraculous action of Jesus worked for a Gentile (see also 8:5-13), her wish is granted because of the greatness of her faith (15:28; see 8:10).

A summary follows. Jesus has moved away to walk by the Sea of Galilee and ascend a mountain to receive a crowd (v. 29). From the region of Tyre and Sidon, Jesus could walk down the western side of the lake through Jewish territory (Capernaum, Tiberius, and so on) or take the eastern shore, associated with the Gentile world (the Decapolis, Gedara, and so on). Matthew's insistence that Jesus "walked by the Sea of Galilee" (v. 29) points to his mission to the Gentiles, first broached as he closed his prologue (1:1 – 4:16). There he located Jesus in Galilee and cites Isaiah 8:23 – 9:1: "the way to the sea, beyond the Jordan, Galilee of the Gentiles. The people who sit in darkness have seen a great light" (4:15-16). What follows 15:29-31 takes place in "the Galilee of the Gentiles."

Jesus' reception and care for the suffering leads to the amazement of the crowds and a glorification of the God of Israel (vv. 30-31). The crowd expresses wonder and praise (v. 31) because the God of Israel has manifested his care for the broken in a Gentile land. The scene is set for Jesus' nourishment of a large crowd on the Gentile side of the lake.[3]

---

3. Contrary to many, I suggest that Matthew (like Mark) presents Jesus as feeding Israel in Matthew 14:13-21 and Gentiles in 15:32-39. See also Schreiner, *Matthew, Disciple and Scribe*, 151-52, 199-201.

The Second Feeding Miracle — Among the Gentiles (15:32–39)

Jesus is moved with pity for the crowd because "they have been with me now for three days and have nothing to eat. I do not want to send them away hungry, for fear they may collapse on the way" (Matt 16:32). They have accompanied the events narrated since Jesus "withdrew to the region of Tyre and Sidon" (15:21)

Several details point to this miraculous feeding as a nourishment of Gentiles. The allusion to Psalm 23:1–5 of verses 18 and 19 is omitted. The crowd sits on the ground (15:35). Jesus' actions transcend this single moment, pointing back to the nourishment of Israel and forward to his final meal with his disciples: "took…gave thanks…broke…and gave them" (see Matt 14:19; 26:26–30). As in 14:19, the disciples make the distribution (15:36). The fragments left over fill seven (not twelve as in 14:20) baskets (15:37). The Greek word for "fragments" (*klasmata*), used in the earliest Church to refer to the eucharistic species, reappears (v. 37; see 14:20). The number "seven" indicates completion, and is applied regularly to the inclusion of the Gentiles among God's people (see, e.g., the mythical origins of the Greek Bible, "the Septuagint" [LXX], the seven deacons established to care for the Greek-speaking believers in Acts 6:1–7). The Greek word used for "baskets" (15:37: *spuridas*) is a generic term for a container, unlike the twelve specifically Jewish wicker baskets (*kophinoi*) that contained the remnants in 14:20. Through these hints, Matthew teaches that the table generated by Jesus' feeding Gentiles remains open. There are seven baskets full of fragments (15:36–37).

The Crisis in the Ministry of the Messiah

First Consequence: The Pharisees and Sadducees Seek a Sign (16:1–4)

Two spectacular feeding miracles are not enough for Israel's leadership. They ask Jesus for a validating sign from heaven to authorize his actions (v. 1). He points to their skill at reading the signs of nature, and their inability to read "the signs of the times" (vv. 2–3).[4] They are an "evil and unfaithful generation" who reject God's Son. The only authorizing sign the he will offer is the sign of Jonah: he will rise after three days (v. 4a).

Second Consequence: The Disciples' "Little Faith," despite Their Understanding (16:5–12)

On leaving the Pharisees and the Sadducees (v. 4b), Jesus reaches the other side of the lake with his disciples. They misunderstand Jesus' use of the expression "leaven" to speak of the teaching of the Pharisees and the Sadducees, just manifested in verses 1–4. They think he is speaking of ordinary bread and are concerned that they have none (vv. 5–7). Jesus accuses their "little faith" (v. 8: *oligopistoi*). After the two spectacular feeding miracles, how can they still be concerned about ordinary bread (vv. 8–10)? Then they understand that he is warning them against the teaching of the Pharisees and the Sadducees (vv. 11–12), but their "littleness of faith" remains. The disciples may have arrived at "understanding," but they are still "of little faith."

---

4. Many important witnesses do not have vv. 2 and 3. It resembles Luke 12:54–56, and later copyists may have inserted it from there.

THE SHAPE OF MATTHEW'S STORY

Third Consequence and Bridge Episode: Peter Accepts that Jesus Is the Son of Man, the Christ, the Son of the Living God. He Is Blessed (16:13–20)

Serving as a "bridge" episode, framed by Jesus' use of the expression "the Son of Man" (vv. 13 and 23), Peter's dual encounter with Jesus at Caesarea Philippi brings 11:2 – 16:23 to a close. It also opens the following section, dedicated to Jesus and his disciples' journey to Jerusalem.

Jesus asks who people say the Son of Man might be (v. 13). The disciples respond that many regard Jesus as a prophetic precursor to the messianic age: John the Baptist, Elijah, Jeremiah, or an eschatological prophet (v. 14). Pressed further on their opinion, Peter makes a perfect confession of faith. In total agreement with the presentation of Jesus in the Gospel's prologue (1:1 – 4:16), and the subsequent positive presentation of Jesus who heals, teaches, and brings in the kingdom of heaven, Peter accepts that Jesus is the Son of Man (v. 13), the Messiah, the Son of the living God (vv. 15–16).

Such faith is not the result of human intuition, but the gift of God. *Peter is blessed because he has been open to that gift* (see 11:25-27). The Greek name for Peter (*petros*) enables a play on the allied Greek word *petra*, used as a nickname meaning "rock." Simon Peter (*petros*) will be the foundation stone (*petra*) for a community of followers of Jesus, a "Church" (*ekklesia*): a group of believers "called forth" (vv. 17–18).

Jewish tradition and practice saw its scribes, Pharisees, and Sadducees as possessing teaching authority. In the Church, Peter is given the authority of binding and loosing, of establishing teaching and caring for the administration of that teaching in the new community (see Isa 22:15–25). What he determines in the community "on earth" will be ratified by the heavenly court (v. 19). For the moment, as Jesus pursues his mission "on earth," there is to be no talk of his being the Messiah (v. 20) because it may be misunderstood. As Matthew shows in the encounter between Jesus and Peter that follows (vv. 21–23), Jesus' messianic status will be achieved through death and resurrection.

Fourth Consequence and Bridge Episode: Peter Does Not Accept that the Son of Man Must Suffer, Die, and Rise. He Is Cursed (16:21–23)

Matthew separates verses 16–20 from 21–23, remarking that "from that time on" (v. 21) Jesus began "to show" his disciples the consequences of Peter's confession of Jesus as "the Messiah, the Son of the living God" (v. 16; see 4:17). The passion prediction of verse 21 is the first of four such predictions (16:21; 18:22–23; 20:17–19; 26:1–2). Jesus is on his way to Jerusalem, the cross, and resurrection (vv. 21–23).

Peter is unwilling to accept that Jesus "must" (the Greek is very strong) go to Jerusalem, to suffer and be slain by the leaders of Israel ("the elders, the chief priests, and the scribes") only to be raised (v. 21). Peter forcibly "takes hold" of Jesus and "rebukes" him. Peter's words (v. 22) reject Jesus' words of verse 21. Jesus turns to Peter *and curses him*. He is a stone that blocks the path to Jerusalem (*skandalon*). He is thus on the side of Satan (see 4:10), unable to accept the strangeness of God's design for his Son (v. 23). Like the disciples of 14:32–33, Peter is a disciple who understands (v. 16) but is unable accept the consequences (vv. 21–22). The "stone" that Jesus blessed (v. 17: *petra*) has become a "stumbling stone" (v. 23: *skandalon*).

Matthew 16:13–23 is made up of two "bridge episodes" linking 11:2 — 20:34. The journey to Jerusalem (16:13 — 20:34) is framed by Peter's confession of faith in 16:13–20 and the

THE SHAPE OF MATTHEW'S STORY

parallel confession of faith of the two blind men in Jericho in 20:29-34. The encounter at Caesarea Philippi also looks back to the question raised by John the Baptist in 11:3: "Are you the one who is to come, or should we look for another?" Matthew has articulated a copious response to that question: Jesus is the Christ, the son of the living God whose destiny is that of the Son of Man (16:13-20). Jesus indicates "from that time on," he must journey to Jerusalem, suffer greatly, be killed, and raised on the third day (vv. 21-23). The way to Jerusalem opens.

> Matthew has told the story of the developing crisis in Jesus' ministry (11:2—16:23) in two stages, opening with the Baptist's question about Jesus' messianic status (11:2-3), turning on the Baptist's death as an anticipation of that of Jesus (14:1-12), and closing with Peter's response to the Baptist's question (16:13-16). Alternative affirmations and rejections of Jesus, including the parable discourse (13:1-52), determine the shape of the first stage (11:2—14:12). Tension between Jesus and the leaders of Israel increases. In the second stage, a feeding of Israel (14:13-21) and a feeding Gentiles (15:32-39), lead the audience through a series of consequences (14:22—15:31; 16:1-23). Jesus continues to be critical of Israel and its traditions, while the disciples show understanding, but "little faith." Peter's confession and subsequent failure serve as a bridge that closes this stage in the story, responding to the Baptist's question (11:2-3), and introducing the theme of the following section: Jesus' journey to Jerusalem "from that time on" (16:21).

Chapter Five

The Messiah's Journey to Jerusalem

Matthew 16:13 – 20:34

The outside limits of the narrative unit of 16:13–20:34 are provided by Peter's christological confession in 16:13–20, matched by the christological confession of the two blind men at Jericho in 20:29-34. The feature of the passage is the triad of passion predictions first articulated in 16:21-23 (see then 18:22-23; 20:17-19). An "overlap" between the account of Jesus' ministry (11:2–16:23) and his journey to Jerusalem (16:13–20:34) is generated by the bridge episodes of 16:13-23 (vv. 13-20 [confession]; vv. 21-23 [passion prediction]).

Peter, James, John (see 4:18-22), and the disciples reject or misunderstand Jesus' passion predictions. Despite their failure, Jesus instructs his disciples, focusing strongly on the call to service and suffering, modeled on the serving and suffering Son of Man (see 20:28).

THE SHAPE OF MATTHEW'S STORY

The Shape of Matthew 16:13—20:34: The Messiah's Journey to Jerusalem

Opening frame: Confession of Peter at Caesarea Philippi (16:13-20)
    The first passion prediction and Peter's failure (16:21-23)
        Jesus' response (16:24—17:20):
            Instruction on the cross (16:24-28)
            The instruction of the transfiguration (17:1-13)
            The instruction of the cure of the epileptic boy (17:14-20)
    The second passion prediction and the disciples' failure (17:22-23)
        Jesus' response (17:24—20:16):
            Opening inner frame: Instruction on the sovereignty of God (17:24-27)
            Instruction on receptivity and the kingdom (18:1-9)
            Instruction on the good shepherd and limitless forgiveness (18:10-35)
            Instruction on marriage (19:1-12)
            Instruction on receptivity and the kingdom (19:13-15)
            Instruction on possessions (19:16-30)
            Closing inner frame: Instruction on the sovereignty of God (20:1-16)
    The third passion prediction and the failure of the sons of Zebedee (20:17-23)
        Jesus' response (20:22-28):
            Instruction of the sons of Zebedee on suffering and service (20:20-23)
            Instruction of the remaining ten of the Twelve on the call to service (20:24-27)
            Christological motivation for suffering and service (20:28)
Closing frame: Confession of the two blind men at Jericho (20:29-34)

The Messiah's Journey to Jerusalem

Opening Frame: Confession of Peter at Caesarea Philippi (16:13–20)

Peter confesses that Jesus is not a precursor but the Christ and the Son of the living God. He is blessed and commissioned for authority in the community of the Church (v. 18).

THE FIRST PASSION PREDICTION AND PETER'S FAILURE (16:21–23)

Peter rejects Jesus' prediction of his journey to Jerusalem, his suffering at the hands of Israel's leaders, his death and resurrection. Taking Jesus aside, he calls on God as he refuses to accept Jesus' prediction (v. 22). He is corrected because he is on the side of Satan (v. 23), despite his appeal to God (v. 22).

JESUS' RESPONSE: INSTRUCTION OF THE DISCIPLES (16:24 – 17:20)

The Instruction on the Cross (16:24–28)

Jesus instructs the disciples that they must take up the cross and follow him to find life (vv. 24–26). Enigmatically, those who lose their lives will find it, and will be rewarded by the Father of Jesus. They do not have long to wait, as some of the disciples hearing Jesus' words will witness the establishment of the Son of Man in his kingdom (vv. 27–28).[1]

---

1. The "timing" of this future experience is challenging (see also Mark 9:1). It must be understood in the light of Jesus' later teaching that only the Father knows when this moment will be (Matt 24:36). For Matthew, it may refer to the disciples' proximate eschatological experience of Jesus' death and resurrection.

THE SHAPE OF MATTHEW'S STORY

The Instruction of the Transfiguration (17:1–13)

Six days after the first passion prediction and the call to the cross, Jesus' transfiguration demonstrates to Peter, James, and John that he is indeed "the Son," and has authority to call his disciples to take up the cross (16:24). His heavenly appearance and the company of Moses and Elijah make it clear that it is a divine summons (vv. 1–3). Peter wants to "hold the moment," but that is not to be (v. 4). They are yet to go up to Jerusalem. A voice from "a bright cloud" (see Exod 24:15–16; 34:5) insists that they are following no less an authority than God's Son. They must listen to him, however challenging a vocation to take up the cross might be (v. 5). Overcome by holy awe (see Dan 8:17; 10:9–11), they prostrate themselves. But "Jesus alone" raises them, insisting, as often in the theophanies of the Hebrew Bible, that they must not fear (vv. 6–7; see Dan 10:12). He instructs them that they are not to proclaim what they have experienced until the full gamut of Jesus' suffering and death has taken place (17:9–13).

The Instruction of the Cure of the Epileptic Boy (17:14–20)

The disciples cannot help a child suffering from epilepsy (vv. 14–16). Using the negative description "faithless and perverse generation," Jesus expresses his frustration with them (v. 17; see 11:16; 12:39, 45; 16:4). His rebuke of the demon heals the boy (vv. 17–18). Answering the disciples' question about their inability to cure the boy, he points to the littleness of their faith. Without faith, they can do nothing; with faith, everything is possible (vv. 19–20).[2]

---

2. Some manuscripts add v. 21. A later addition from Mark 9:29, it should be omitted.

Peter, who rightly confesses faith in Jesus (16:13-20), does not accept God's design that will lead to his suffering, death, and resurrection (vv. 21-23). Despite this failure, Jesus instructs his fragile disciples that they are called to follow their Messiah, authoritatively manifested and proclaimed as the Son of God (17:1-13), through suffering, death (16:24-28), and faith (17:19-20). Discipleship is a call to an unquestioning openness to God who makes all things possible (17:14-20).

THE SECOND PASSION PREDICTION AND THE DISCIPLES' FAILURE (17:22-23)

Gathered with his disciples in Galilee, Jesus predicts his forthcoming passion: the Son of Man will be handed over to men, and they will kill him. But on the third day he will be raised (vv. 22-23a). The disciples cannot accept God's plan for his Son: "And they were overwhelmed with grief" (v. 23b). They understand what lies ahead but are unwilling to accept it.

JESUS' RESPONSE: INSTRUCTION OF THE DISCIPLES (17:24 – 20:16)

This instruction follows Mark 9:33 – 10:31, but includes new elements, especially the frame of 17:24-27 and 20:1-16.

Opening Frame: Instruction on the Sovereignty of God (17:24-27)

In Capernaum, Jesus' hometown, he is interrogated about paying the temple tax (vv. 24-25a). God's Son, recently revealed at the transfiguration (vv. 1-8), pays the tax as part of his perfect response to the Law (see 5:17–19). However, as a "subject," and not a "foreigner," he has no such obligation (25b–26). Jesus instructs Peter to take the first fish of a catch and find in its mouth a coin to pay double the temple tax. Jesus' status as the Son of God (16:13–18; 17:1–8) and God's absolute sovereignty over nature and the affairs of humankind (17:24–27) have been stated (17:24–27). God is a Father who does everything for his Son, seeing to it that the Law's requirements are met. "The whole point is that *God's children are free with respect to God their Father*."[3] The Son is free to respond to the lordship of the Father.

Instruction on Receptivity and the Kingdom (18:1–9)

The disciples ask who is the greatest in the kingdom of heaven, seeking the affirmation of worldly success and honor (18:1). Calling a child, Jesus asks the disciples to "turn and become like little children." The summons to "turn" (*straphēte*) is a call to reverse their current value system. In that system, a child has no status. The disciples will not enter the kingdom — much less achieve greatness — without the humility and receptive openness to God that marks a child's innocent lack of self-concern. The repetition of the verb "to receive" in verse 5 insists that disciples must welcome all who come. Matthew refers to other members of the community as "one such child" (*hen paidion toiouto*; see also 19:13–14), described in the immediate context as "one of these little ones" (*hena tōn mikrōn toutōn*; see vv. 6, 10, 14). Receptivity of others is nothing less than the reception of Jesus (18:5; see 25:31–46).

Damaging "one of these little ones" leads to destruction (vv. 6–7). Jesus instructs disciples on dramatic inner-community dangers. The nature of the damage possibly

---

3. Davies and Allison, *Saint Matthew*, 2:741. Emphasis in original.

done to a member of the community — by a member of the community — is covered by the verb *skandalizō*, an expression that describes several possible actions, from scandal that comes from bad behavior to despising or not recognizing members of the community. Peter's rejection of Jesus' first passion prediction has led to his being called "a stumbling block" (16:23: *skandalon*). The command to receptivity must be heeded. The severity of the punishment is paralleled by the radical nature of the cure. Everyone has two hands, feet, and eyes, all of which might damage "these little ones." We can survive with only one; better to have only one than be thrown into Gehenna with both, having damaged a member of the community (vv. 8-9).

Instruction on the Good Shepherd and Limitless Forgiveness (18:10-35)

The antithesis of the scandal and division described in verses 1-9 follows, with the parable of the lost sheep (vv. 10-14), the treatment of a member of the community who sins (vv. 15-20), and the parable of the unforgiving servant (vv. 21-35). The question posed in the parable, what person leaves ninety-nine of his hundred sheep in the hills and goes in search of the stray (vv. 10-12), deserves the response: "No one!" Against all such "common sense," the will of the Father in heaven is that all be saved, that not "one of these little ones be lost" (v. 14). Sin happens, and a community of followers of Jesus is instructed on how it must be resolved: between the offended and the offender (v. 15), before two witnesses (v. 16), or before the whole community (v. 17a: *ekklesia*). When all fails, "then treat him as you would a Gentile or a tax collector" (v. 17a). For the First Gospel, this does not point to rejection. Matthew is a tax collector, called to be one of the Twelve (see 9:9-13; 10:3).

THE SHAPE OF MATTHEW'S STORY

The First Gospel climaxes with the command to take the good news to all nations (28:16-20). Jesus eats with tax collectors (9:10-11) and is attacked because he is their friend (11:19). Unreserved compassion and forgiveness, practiced by a community bound together in prayer and action, will be matched by a heavenly forgiveness. The risen Jesus is in their midst (vv. 18-20; see 1:23; 28:20).

Unreserved compassion is demonstrated by the behavior of the king in the parable on the kingdom of heaven that Jesus uses to respond to the stunned question from Peter: "How often must I forgive him?" There is no quantity that can measure forgiveness (vv. 21-22). The king forgives a servant an impossible debt, "moved with compassion" (vv. 23-27). But the servant's compassion does not match his king's leadership. He is thus punished by an angry king (vv. 28-34). The prayer that Jesus taught his disciples, asking their Father to forgive them as they forgive their brothers and sisters (6:12) provides the key to the quality of compassion and receptivity in the community: "So will my heavenly Father do to you, unless each of you forgives his brother from his heart" (18:35).

Instruction on Marriage (19:1-12)

In a rare interruption of the series of encounters between Jesus and the disciples, leaving Galilee, crossing the Jordan, and entering Judea, Jesus is questioned by the Pharisees (19:1-3). The discussion may be between Jesus and the Pharisees, but Matthew continues to speak to his audience about life in community. Cutting across all contemporary discussions of possible motives for divorce, based on Deuteronomy 24:1-4, Jesus returns to God's design for the union between a man and a woman in marriage, which no one should separate (vv. 4-9). Jesus only allows the separation of a marriage that is "unlawful" (v. 9; see 5:31-32). The Greek word *porneia* can be applied to many unacceptable sexual relationships. As Matthew addresses his Jewish Christian community beginning to receive Gentiles into their midst, he recognizes that some may have come into that situation already involved in a relationship that was unacceptable. Such relationships would be judged as *porneia* by Matthew's largely Jewish-Christian community. For example, Greco-Roman culture allowed marriage with close relatives (what we call consanguinity), but this was unacceptable in Jewish marriage practice. In those cases, he allows separation.

This "inner-community" situation is further clarified by the disciples' shocked reaction to the prohibition of divorce. If it is not possible to divorce within the community, then they would be better off not to marry (v. 10). The situation dealt with in verses 4–9 is still in view. Jesus agrees that such a marital ethic is difficult and must be accepted as a gift (v. 11). But he goes further. Dissolved marriage situations may call for a life without a spouse. Some believing followers of Jesus will remain unmarried because of the overpowering gift of the kingdom in their lives (vv. 11–12). They refrain from marriage "because of" the kingdom that determines all their decisions and actions.[4]

Instruction on Receptivity and the Kingdom (19:13–15)

The instruction on receptivity, found in 18:1–9, returns before Jesus broaches the issue of riches and possessions.

---

4. The Greek preposition *dia*, followed by the accusative case (*tēn basileian*) means "because of." The decision to remain unmarried is a consequence of the overwhelming experience of the kingdom.

THE SHAPE OF MATTHEW'S STORY

As Jesus welcomes, blesses, and prays with children (vv. 13a, 15; see 18:2, 3, 4, 5), the disciples object. Children are an unrecognized part of society. Yet Jesus accepts, blesses, and prays with them, "for the kingdom of heaven belongs to such as these" (vv. 13b–14). The "children" of 18:1–5 and 19:13–15, along with the "little ones" of 18:6–9, portray the childlike receptivity required from true disciples of Jesus. The kingdom belongs to them (v. 14).

Instruction on Possessions (19:16–30)

The rich young man (v. 20) models an attitude that opposes Jesus' instruction on receptivity. He asks Jesus, "What must I do to gain eternal life" (v. 16). He has observed all the social commandments that a rich man might be tempted to offend (vv. 18–21). His law-abiding goodness recognized, Jesus asks him to make the extra step, to progress from his quality Jewish life, to rid himself of anything that may stand between himself and a following of Jesus. He is called to be "perfect," to become part of a community that attempts to live the agenda Jesus established in the Sermon on the Mount (see 5:48; 19:21). Possessions stand between this man and an unconditional "following" of Jesus (19:21; see 6:24). He fails to respond to Jesus' call, "for he had many possessions" (v. 22). It is not a question of what he can do to gain eternal life (v. 16), but what the receptive following of Jesus can do for him (v. 21).

Jesus addresses the disciples directly (vv. 23–30). His challenge to the rich young man that he rid himself of all his possessions appears impossible. As Jesus himself admits, a camel cannot pass through the eye of a needle (vv. 23–24). One could say the same thing about Jesus' earlier instruction to his community on earlier the challenge of Jesus' teaching on marriage (vv. 1–12). It is impossible to live in a situation where divorce is not allowed. The astonished dis-

The Messiah's Journey to Jerusalem

ciples agree: "Who then can be saved?" (v. 25). Jesus is calling his followers to place their trust elsewhere, beyond what appears humanly reasonable. For God, even the impossible is possible (v. 26).

Peter continues the questioning, asking what the disciples who have left everything will receive (v. 27). Those who have given up possessions (including the intimacies of family life) in following Jesus will accompany the enthroned Son of Man at the end of this era. They will judge the twelve tribes of Israel. They will be rewarded one hundredfold and inherit eternal life (v. 29). The established order of honor and success will be reversed under God's sovereignty (v. 30).

Closing Frame: Instruction on the Sovereignty of God (20:1-16)

Without any introduction, Jesus tells a parable on the reversal of established order in the kingdom: "The kingdom of heaven is like a landowner…" (20:1). When laborers who have worked in the vineyard "from dawn" (v. 1), from "about nine o'clock" (v. 3), from "around noon" (v. 5a), from "around three o'clock" (v. 5b), and a final group summoned at "about five o'clock" (v. 6), all receive the same recompense. Who behaves like this (see 18:12)? The lord in the kingdom of heaven responds, "Am I not free to do as I wish with my own money? Are you envious because I am generous" (v. 15)? The closing passage in the long sequence of Jesus' instruction of his disciples (17:24—20:16) that follows the second passion prediction (17:22-23), highlights the incomprehensible goodness of God (20:1-16), and "the scandalous nature of God's grace."[5]

---

5. Garland, *Reading Matthew*, 206.

THE SHAPE OF MATTHEW'S STORY

Matthew 17:24—20:16 opens and closes with passages that indicate God's sovereignty, manifested in his Son's behavior (17:24-27) and in the reversal of established order that is the hallmark of the kingdom of heaven (20:1-16). Jesus' instruction of his disciples from 18:1—19:30 has focused intensely on community issues: the call for receptivity (18:1-9; 19:13-15), limitless forgiveness (18:15-35), marriage (19:1-12), and possessions (19:16-30). The perfection of God's Law (see 5:17-20, 48), a radical reversal of the accepted order within the community of Jesus makes sense in the light of the message that lies at the heart of 17:24—20:16: "For human beings this is impossible, but for God all things are possible" (19:26; see also 17:20).

THE THIRD PASSION PREDICTION AND THE FAILURE OF THE SONS OF ZEBEDEE (20:17-23)

Jesus' third prediction of his forthcoming death and resurrection is marked by an indication that he is journeying with his disciples to Jerusalem, and that he reveals his future only to them (20:17). Despite the detail of Jesus' prediction, and the only mention of "crucifixion" across the three predictions, the mother of the sons of Zebedee makes a request. Her sons have not understood the nature of the kingdom. They fail to accept their future as disciples of Jesus (see 17:24-38). Misunderstanding the promise of the disciples' future role on thrones of judgment (19:28), she asks that her sons have positions of honor and power when Jesus establishes his messianic kingdom in Jerusalem (v. 21).

The Messiah's Journey to Jerusalem

JESUS' RESPONSE *(20:22-28)*

Instruction of the Sons of Zebedee on Suffering and Service (20:22-23)

Jesus addresses the two sons, informing them that they have not understood what they are seeking. He asks whether they are prepared to drink the cup that he will drink (v. 22). To their confident response that they can, he affirms that such a future lies ahead of them. But positions of honor on the right and left of Jesus in Jerusalem will be granted by the Father: to two revolutionaries (v. 23; see 27:38). Matthew's audience senses the poignancy of this encounter, especially as the sons of Zebedee had possibly been slain by the time the First Gospel appeared (see Acts 12:2 for Herod's execution of James).

Instruction of the Remaining Ten on the Call to Service (20:24-27)

The "other ten" are angry because they suspect the sons of Zebedee are jockeying for positions of power in the forthcoming establishment of the messianic kingdom (v. 24). They also fail to accept the prediction of verses 17-19. They are not to be like other authorities; they are called to be servants (*diakonoi*) and slaves (*douloi*) (vv. 25-27).

Christological Motivation for the Call to Suffering and Service (20:28)

The challenge of discipleship is the call to suffering and service. Jesus instructs his disciples that he is not an

THE SHAPE OF MATTHEW'S STORY

indifferent lawgiver. His own life, ministry, death, and resurrection provide the christological motivation for all that Jesus asks of his disciples across 16:21—20:28. Disciples are "followers" of Jesus. He leads the way: "The Son of Man did not come to be served (*diakonēthēnai*) but to serve (*diakonēsai*) and to give his life as a ransom for many" (v. 28).

> Jesus' three passion predictions (16:21-23; 17:22-23; 20:17-21) have been followed by the disciples' failure (16:22-23; 17:23b; 20:20-21). He responds with perseverance, instructing them on the requirements for authentic discipleship: receptivity (17:14-20; 18:1-9; 19:13-15) and the need for suffering and cross (16:24-28; 20:22-23, 24-27). They are manifested in the quality of the life of the community in those areas that touch human experience most profoundly: forgiveness (18:10-35), marriage (19:1-12), and possessions (19:16-30). These qualities turn accepted social and political values upside down (18:1-5; 19:30; 20:16). God's sovereignty over all things matters most (17:24-27; 20:1-16). With God, all things are possible (17:20; 19:26).

Closing Frame: Confession of the Two Blind Men at Jericho (20:29-34)

This brief episode looks in several directions. Its location at Jericho informs the audience that Jesus is approaching Jerusalem. The blind men's confession that Jesus is "Lord, Son of David" (vv. 30, 31) looks back to Peter's confession at Caesarea Philippi (16:13-20), thus framing 16:13—20:34. The two blind men demonstrate the unconditional commitment to Jesus that—until this stage in the story—the other disciples have not achieved. Despite being rebuked by the crowd, they twice call on Jesus as "Lord, Son of David" (vv. 30-31). Responding to Jesus' question about their hopes, they ask that their eyes be opened (v. 33). Personifying the compassion that Jesus has asked of his disciples (18:10-35), "moved with pity" he touched their eyes (v. 34a). There is more to "seeing" in this episode that regaining vision. "Immediately...they followed him" (v. 34). They join him in his journey to Jerusalem and what has been promised will take place there (20:18), something the disciples have either resisted (16:22-23; 17:23b) or misunderstood (20:20-22). Jesus heals blindness and transforms disciples into "followers."

> Jesus' threefold prediction of his forthcoming passion, death, and resurrection in Jerusalem (16:21-23; 17:22-23; 20:17-21) is the feature of his journey to the city. It began in 16:13-23 (see v. 21). After each prediction disciples fail to understand or accept that the events in Jerusalem will mark Jesus' unconditional response to the design of his Father (see 26:39). Failure leads to Jesus' instructions on what it means to "follow" him. The first (16:24—17:20) and third (20:22-27) parts of that instruction focus on the call to suffering and the cross, culminating in Jesus' self-revelation as the Son of Man who came not to be served but to serve and to give his life as a ransom for many (20:28). The long central section (17:24—20:16) deals with the marks of a community committed to the following of Jesus: receptivity, forgiveness, marriage, and possessions. None of this is possible without the recognition of an instruction that frames the middle section: the sovereignty of God (17:24-27; 20:1-16). With God, everything is possible (17:20; 19:26).

CHAPTER SIX

The Messiah's Death and Resurrection in Jerusalem

Matthew 21:1 – 28:15

Jesus' approach to Jerusalem (21:1-9) and his physical entry into the city (vv. 10-11) open Matthew's treatment of Jesus' only presence in Jerusalem. He will not leave the city until he returns to the mountain in Galilee as the risen one (28:16-20). Three stages mark 21:1 – 28:15:

>   Jesus' entry and ministry in Jerusalem:
>   21:1 – 25:46
>   Jesus' passion and death: 26:1 – 27:66
>   The aftermath of Jesus death: 28:1-15

JESUS' ENTRY AND MINISTRY IN JERUSALEM: 21:1 – 25:46

Matthew's location of Jesus in Jerusalem, established in 21:1-11, provides the narrative backbone to 21:12 – 25:46. In the Jerusalem temple, Israel's institutions (21:12-22) and leadership (21:23 – 23:39) are judged. Gazing at the splendors

The Messiah's Death and Resurrection in Jerusalem

of the temple (24:1), Jesus announces God's eschatological judgment of the nations (24:1 – 25:46).

The Shape of Matthew 21:1–25:46: Jesus in Jerusalem

Jesus *enters* Jerusalem: 21:1-11
Jesus *enters* and *exits* the temple: the cursed fig tree: 21:12-22
Jesus in the temple: 21:23—23:39
    Parables that punish the leaders of Israel:
        Introduction: the question of Jesus' authority: 21:23-27
        The parable of the two sons: 21:28-32
        The parable of the tenants: 21:33-46
        The parable of the wedding feast: 22:1-14
    Conflicts with the leaders of Israel:
        Conflict with the Pharisees: 22:15-22
        Conflict with the Sadducees: 22:23-33
        The greatest commandment: 22:34-40
        David's son: 22:41-46
    Condemnation of the Scribes and Pharisees: 23:1-39
Jesus leaves the temple: 24:1—25:46
    The end of Jerusalem: 24:1-28
    The end of the world: 24:29-35
    The need for watchfulness: 24:36—25:30
        The unknown day and hour: 24:36-44
        The faithful or unfaithful servant: 24:45-51
        The ten bridesmaids: 25:1-13
        The talents: 25:14-30
    The judgment of the nations: 25:31-46

THE SHAPE OF MATTHEW'S STORY

Jesus Enters Jerusalem: 21:1-11

From the village of Bethphage Jesus sends two disciples to prepare for his entry into Jerusalem by bringing an ass and her colt (vv. 1-2, 6). Their authority is "the Lord has need of them" (v. 3). God is directing these events; the prophecies of Isaiah 62:11 and Zechariah 9:9 are fulfilled (v. 5). The entry into Jerusalem and its consequences are not the result of accident or fate. They fulfill God's design.

The Jerusalem crowd proclaims the arrival of the messianic Son of David, the one who comes in the name of the Lord (vv. 7-9). But his entry as a meek king, riding on a colt, the foal of a beast of burden (v. 5), points this acclamation in an unexpected direction. "The whole city was shaken (*eseistha*)" at his entry (v. 10). This Greek verb, generally used in association with an earthquake, will accompany the events of Jesus' death (27:51) and the terror of the guards at Jesus' empty tomb (28:4). The eschatological turning point of the ages has begun (see also 8:24). Wondering who this man might be, the crowds accept that he is a prophet from Nazareth in Galilee (vv. 10-11), returning to the name announced in 2:23: "He shall be called a Nazorean."

Jesus Enters and Exits the Temple: The Cursed Fig Tree: 21:12-22

Jesus shuts down practices essential to the cultic activity of the temple: the exchange of coins so that no effigies were taken into the temple area, and the sale of doves used for sacrifices (v. 12). He claims the temple as his own ("my house"), a house of prayer to God, not of human commerce (v. 13; see Isa 56:7; 60:7). His actions lead to acclaim from the blind, the lame, and the children, traditionally prohibited from temple worship (vv. 14-15; see 2 Sam 5:8). The chief priests and the scribes ask him to stop this recognition. But

The Messiah's Death and Resurrection in Jerusalem

the praise fulfills Israel's Scriptures (Ps 8:3; see 11:25). Jesus leaves the city and goes to Bethany.

The following day, Jesus curses a fig tree, long used as a symbol for Israel (see Hos 9:10, 16–17; Mic 4:4; 7:1; Jer 8:13; 24:1–10; 29:17; Zech 3:10). Jesus' break with Israel and its temple is radical: "May no fruit ever come from you again" (v. 19). The disciples' amazement is resolved by Jesus' teaching that access to God is through faith and prayer (vv. 21–22; see 7:7–11). Faith could produce the physical disappearance of the temple, "this mountain," cast into the sea (v. 21). Writing after the destruction of Jerusalem and its temple, Matthew's Jesus points to prayer and faith that can move mountains, even the temple mountain (see 17:20).

> The journey to Jerusalem comes to an end (21:1–11). A series of "endings" begins as the centralized temple cult of Israel is brought to a standstill, replaced by the universal (the blind, the lame, and the children) possibility of prayer and faith (21:12–22).

Jesus Enters the Temple: The Question of Jesus' Authority: 21:23–27

As Jesus enters the temple, the chief priests and the elders of the people ask for the source of his authority (vv. 1–11) to act as he did (vv. 12–17). Authority comes from one teacher to another (see John 7:15). Where does Jesus' authority come from (Matt 21:23)? Beginning a series of encounters between himself and various groups of religious leaders (see 22:15–46), he reduces them to silence by raising the question of the origins of the message of John the Baptist (vv. 24–25a). Caught in the horns of a dilemma between saying what they think and unsettling the crowd that regarded the Baptist as a prophet (vv. 25b-26), the discussion stalemates.

PARABLES THAT PUNISH ISRAEL: 21:28 – 22:14

The Parable of the Two Sons (21:28-32)

Jesus leads the chief priests and the elders (see v. 23) to an admission that it is not the son who promises to work in the vineyard and does nothing, but the son who rebelled but "changed his mind," who does the father's will (vv. 28-31a). Matthew links the parable with the discussion of the authority of John the Baptist (vv. 23-27). Tax collectors and prostitutes believed John the Baptist and repented; Israel's religious leaders did not (see 3:5-7). They promise much, but they do not accept God's prophet (vv. 31b-32a; see 3:3). Tax collectors and prostitutes have "changed their minds." The sight of this phenomenon makes no impression on the leaders of Israel. They do not "change their minds" (v. 32b). Their rejection of John the Baptist indicates that they are locked into a closed system that has no place for God (the "Father") and his Son. Others enter the kingdom ahead of them.

The Parable of the Tenants (21:33-46)

Jesus tells of a vineyard, another symbol for Israel (see Isa 5:1-7; Ps 80:8-13; Jer 2:21). Israel's leaders had an obligation to care for the vineyard that has been leased to them (Matt 21:33). The landowner has sent his prophets and saints seeking to restore Israel's fruits to its rightful owner. But its leadership has repulsed them, abused them, and slain them (vv. 34-36). He even sent his son, but they executed him outside the vineyard, a reference to Jesus' execution (vv. 37-39; see 27:32-33; Heb 13:12; Rev 11:8). Jesus changes his

The Messiah's Death and Resurrection in Jerusalem

description of the "landowner" (v. 33: *oikodespotēs*). Asked what the Lord (v. 40: *kyrios*) should do to such tenants, the leaders prophesy their own future (v. 40).[1] Matthew's audience recalls the recent destruction of Israel and its temple during the Jewish War of 65–70 CE. The Lord will destroy of the wicked tenants, handing over the vineyard to "other tenants" who will respond fruitfully to God "at the proper times" (v. 41).

Jesus points out that God's design will not be thwarted by the leaders' rejection of him. Fulfilling the Scriptures (Ps 118:22–23), the rejected stone will become the cornerstone of a structure that will emerge from the execution of the Son. Their place in the kingdom of God will be taken from the leaders of Israel and given to another people. Fruits of the vineyard have been transformed into "the fruits of the kingdom" (v. 43). The chief priests and the Pharisees recognize that he has been speaking of them but are reduced to silence out of fear for the crowds who recognize Jesus as a prophet (vv. 45–46; see 21:26).[2]

The Parable of the Wedding Feast (22:1–14)

A further parable directed to the leaders (21:23) uses an image that continues the message of the parable of the tenants (22:15–22). A king summons invited guests to a wedding feast, a symbol of the messianic age (see Isa 25:6–8; 54:4–8; 62:4–5), for his son (Matt 22:1). The guests refuse to come (v. 3). He sends other servants and describes the feast. But the guests ignore the invitation, mistreating and slaying the servants (vv. 4–7; see 21:34–35). The king responds by burning and destroying their city (v. 7), matching the

---

1. The NABRE misses this, rendering the different words in vv. 33 and 40 as "landowner."
2. Most critics regard v. 44 as an insertion of Luke 20:18 by early copyists.

destruction of Jerusalem hinted at in 21:41–42. The king fills the halls with guests from the roads and the streets, the bad and the good alike (see 13:47; see also 13:24–30). The eschatological nature of this messianic age, however, brings judgment. Greeting a guest as "my friend," he asks why he is not wearing a wedding garment (22:11–12). It is not enough to "be there." Even among the Gentiles, a change of heart (see 3:2; 4:17), doing the will of God (12:50), is required. The sullen silence of the guest leads to exclusion from the feast and punishment. Jews and Gentiles are summoned to the wedding feast of the king. Only those who live a life of good deeds (see 7:21–23), responding worthily to God's gifts, will be granted final participation (22:13–14).[3]

> With authority (21:23–27), Jesus tells a series of parables that chastise the failure of Jewish leadership to respond to the promises and invitations of God. Their privileges will be taken from them, and unexpectedly given to others (21:28—22:14).

CONFLICTS WITH THE LEADERS OF ISRAEL: 22:15–46

Conflict with the Pharisees (22:15–22)

The Pharisees attempt to "entrap" Jesus in his teaching. They send their disciples (strict Law-abiders), with Herodians (associated with corrupt Roman authority) (vv. 15–16a). After praise, they ask a question about the payment of the tax to Caesar (vv. 16b–17). They are attempting to place Jesus in a

---

3. Some suggest that the king would have provided a wedding garment and is thus outraged that it is not being worn. See Craig L., *Matthew*, The New American Commentary (Nashville: Broadman Press, 1992), 328–29.

winless situation. Refusal to pay the tax means disloyalty to the agenda of the Herodians but accepting to pay the tax is disloyal to the Pharisees' understanding of the uniqueness of Israel. Jesus' response opens with an attack on their malice, calling them "hypocrites" for the first time (v. 18; see 23:13-36). They produce a Roman coin marked with the effigy of Caesar (vv. 19-20). They have desecrated the temple by bearing the effigy of a human authority (see 21:12). Jesus now has the ascendency, able to command them to render to Caesar what belongs to Caesar (the coin and the tax), and to God what is God's (the "house of prayer" [21:13]; see 4:1-11) (v. 21). They depart, amazed (v. 22).

Conflict with the Sadducees (22:23-33)

Motivated by their rejection of an afterlife (v. 23), the Sadducees question Jesus' beliefs through the example of a woman who had seven deceased husbands before her own death. If there is a resurrection and afterlife, "whose wife will she be" (vv. 24-29)? Jesus' response accuses them of ignorance of the Scriptures and the power of God. Beyond this life God's power transforms the human condition. The human and social necessity of marriage is no longer in place (v. 30). Their ignorance of the Scriptures is shown by their misunderstanding of God's revelation to Moses at the burning bush. By the time of Moses, the patriarchs, Abraham, Isaac, and Jacob, had all died. But the God revealed to Moses is the God of Abraham, Isaac, and Jacob (Exod 3:6). They must be living, as "He is not the God of the dead but of the living" (v. 32). The crowds are astonished at his teaching (v. 33).

The Greatest Commandment (22:34-40)

The silencing of the Sadducees leads a gathering of the Pharisees to have one of their group test Jesus over an often-asked issue: the greatest commandment of the Law (vv. 34-36). Jesus responds by citing Deuteronomy 6:5, the most powerful articulation of Israel's call to love and serve the God of Israel with the whole person (heart, soul, and mind). To this Jesus adds the love of neighbor as equally important, citing Leviticus 19:18 (v. 39). There is no objection to Jesus' interpretation of the Law (see 5:17; 7:12), possibly already part of Jewish thought known by Matthew's audience (v. 40).

David's Son (22:41-46)

Jesus tests the Pharisees by asking whose son is the Messiah. They respond that the Messiah is the son of David (vv. 41-42). Jesus' unexpected response indicates his superior understanding of Israel's Scriptures. Citing Psalm 110:1, Jesus takes it for granted that the Spirit-filled David is the author of the Psalm. David refers to the Messiah as "my lord," promised to sit at God's right hand, having conquered all his enemies (v. 43). If David calls the Messiah "my lord," he cannot only be his son. For Matthew, the Christ is the son of David (see 1:1; 21:9, 15), but he is more: the son of the living God (15:33; 16:16), whose destiny is the destiny of the Son of Man (16:13-16, 27-28; 17:12, 22; 19:28; 20:17-19; 24:29-31, 37-41, 44; 25:31; 26:1-2). His suffering and ultimate vindication had already been described in Daniel 7:1-25 (see vv. 13-14).

Jesus has reduced the Pharisees and the crowds to amazement (vv. 22, 33). He has corrected them in his interpretation of Israel's Scriptures (vv. 31-33; 37-40; 43-45). He has stopped the cultic activity of the temple and replaced it with prayer and faith (21:1-22). He has silenced the Pharisees and the Sadducees and reduced the crowd to amazement (21:23 – 22:45). Jesus is the master of the situation: "No one was able to answer him a word, nor from that day on did anyone dare to ask him any more questions" (22:46). As with his use of intercalations marked by positive and negative responses to Jesus, the conflicts between Jesus and Israel's religious institutions call for a response from Matthew's audience: Jesus or the leaders of Israel?

> Jesus systematically reduces the major religious institutions to silence: the temple, the Pharisees, Sadducees, and the Herodians. From that day on no one dared to ask him any more questions.

CONDEMNATION OF THE SCRIBES AND PHARISEES *(23:1–39)*

Although only Jesus speaks across 23:1–39, the passage does not end in a typical discourse fashion (see 7:28; 11:1; 13:53; 19:1; 26:1). It is aimed at three different audiences: to the crowds and disciples (12:1–12), seven "woes" spoken directly to the Scribes and the Pharisees (vv. 13–36), and a final lament over Jerusalem (vv. 37–39).

Writing for a Jewish Christian community late in the first century (c. 85–90 CE), Matthew addresses the broken relationship between his community and the local Jewish community. The passion of Jesus' attack in 23:1–39 was generated by at least two experiences.

1. After 70 CE, a gradual "parting of the ways" developed between the Jewish community that did not accept Jesus as the Christ, and the small Jewish Christian community that did. Judaism was gradually being restored by their leaders. Matthew's community maintained its Jewish roots but was beginning to go its own way as followers of Jesus

Christ, accepting Gentile converts, fruit of a mission to "all the nations" (see 28:16–20).

2. In the late 80s of the first century, the Scribes and the Pharisees were not listening to the First Gospel, but early Christians were. They believed that the crucified Jesus the Nazorean (see 2:23; 21:11) was the Christ. They inherited Jewish traditions and practices for which many had sacrificed their lives as recently as the time of the Maccabean wars (c. 160–67 BCE). The Christian community strove for a lifestyle that did not abandon the traditions of Israel. But Jesus claimed a perfection of the teaching of Moses through love, even of one's enemies (5:1–48; 22:34–40). Families, friends, and coreligionists in the Jewish synagogue probably challenged them as they parted company.

The harshness of 23:1–39 is not primarily an attack on the leaders of Israel, but a guide to wavering Christians who might wish to return to the much-loved religious practices of Judaism. In verses 8–12, Jesus speaks to "the crowds and his disciples." He insists, "This is not how it should be among you." As throughout his story, Matthew is asking the members of his audience where they stand.

Jesus Addresses the Crowds and His Disciples (23:1–12)

The Scribes and Pharisees rightly exercise a role as authentic teachers, but they do not practice what they preach (vv. 1–3). Their hypocrisy should not be imitated. They impose burdens but offer no support, unlike Jesus, whose yoke is easy and burden light (v. 4; see 11:30). Good deeds are important (see 7:21–27; 21:28–32), but they are not to be paraded as virtue and used to occupy positions of privilege (vv. 5–8; see 6:1–18). The Christian community is not the place for titles of honor, but a place of service in imitation of their one "master," the messiah who came not to be served but to serve, and to lay down his life for others (see 20:28). A reversal of accepted practices will take place at the final judgment (23:12).

Jesus Addresses the Scribes and the Pharisees (23:13–36)

Through seven "woes" (the opposite of beatitudes), Jesus points to the failures of the Scribes and the Pharisees to respond to God's designs, made known by Jesus. The crowds and the disciples (v. 1) have not been dismissed. They hear Jesus' words against the Scribes and the Pharisees who lock people out of the kingdom, contrasting the role of Peter, who has the keys to grant entry (v. 13; see 16:19). The Scribes and the Pharisees compete with Matthew's community for members but offer only destruction (v. 15: "a child of Gehenna"). They have developed a casuistry that depends on the swearing of oaths, but all oaths must entail witness before God (vv. 16–22). Tithing was part of the Torah tradition (Lev 27:30–33; Deut 14:22–29). Jesus does not condemn their tithing, but their concern with minutiae ("mint, and dill and cumin"). Lost in the minutiae (the gnat), they neglect the central values of Torah (swallowing the camel). Jesus seeks mercy, and not sacrifice (vv. 23–24; see 9:13; 12:7).

The final "woes" return to the charge of hypocrisy: ritual cleansings that are not reflected in their "plunder and self-indulgence" (vv. 25–26), and a whitening of tombstones so that a passerby might be warned against ritual impurity through contact with the dead. Meanwhile, the Scribes and the Pharisees inwardly seethe with evildoing (vv. 27–28). The seventh woe (vv. 29–36) continues the theme of tombs, alluding to the suffering of Christian prophets. The Jewish leaders create monuments for prophets and wise men whom their ancestors have slain (vv. 29-33). Recalling the message of the parables of the tenants (21:41) and the wedding feast (22:7), they are children who continue the practices of earlier generations. They persecute, kill, and crucify prophets, wise men, and scribes that Jesus sends. The punishment for the crime of shedding of righteous blood, from Abel (Gen 4:1-16) till the recent slaying of Zechariah, son of Barachiah will fall upon them (Matt 23:34-35). The recent experience of the Jewish War indicates that punishment has "come upon this generation" (v. 36).

Lament over Jerusalem (23:37-39)

God's care for his people and their city, manifested in Jesus' desire to gather their children as a brooding hen, has not disappeared (v. 37). Their rejection of Jesus will lead to the desolation and destruction of the temple. The city will not see Jesus again until he makes his eschatological entry as judge (see 16:28; 24:29-31; 25:31-46; 26:64). These are Jesus' final words in Jerusalem before the passion. Some in Jerusalem will cry out the truth: "Blessed is he who comes in the name of the Lord" (23:38-39). "For Matthew the drama of Israel was not yet concluded."[4]

> The attack on the Scribes and the Pharisees in 23:1-39 is directed to the crowd and the disciples (23:1). Most accusations do not reflect first-century Judaism. They were generated by the rhetoric of Matthew's response to the breakdown between post-War Judaism and earliest Christianity. Jesus' words can be applied to all institutions. "Hypocrisy and the imposition of burdens upon others that

---

4. Senior, *Matthew*, 264-65.

The Messiah's Death and Resurrection in Jerusalem

one is unwilling to bear oneself are failings from which no religious tradition can think itself exempt."[5]

JESUS LEAVES THE TEMPLE: MATTHEW 24:1 – 25:46

The End of Jerusalem, the World, and the Coming of the Son of Man: Matthew 24:1-35

Matthew follows Mark 13:1-37, but he devotes more sustained focus on the end of all things. Jesus leaves the temple area, locating himself and his disciples in a geographic situation where they can look upon the buildings (v. 1). Jesus predicts that all will be thrown down (v. 2). Seated on the Mount of Olives the disciples ask *when* this will happen, and *what signs* will indicate the end of the age (v. 3).[6]

The scene is set for the discourse on the end of Jerusalem (vv. 4-28), the end of the world (vv. 29-35), a series of instructions on the need to be watchful (24:36 – 25:30), and a description of the final judgment of the nations (25:31-46). The discourse of 24:4 – 25:46 is more than "discourse." Jesus instructs his disciples on what lies ahead of them, and how they are to meet future challenges. It is Jesus' testament for his disciples.[7]

The End of Jerusalem and Beyond: Matthew 24:4-28

Prior to, and even during, the struggle for Jerusalem in 70 CE, false prophets emerged making claims about the advent of the Messiah (vv. 4-5, 11, 23-24, 26; see Josephus,

---

5. Byrne, *Lifting the Burden*, 177.
6. There are numerous suggestions concerning the literary shape of 24:1 – 25:46. The following is influenced by Schweizer, *Matthew*, 448-82.
7. See Davies and Allison, *Saint Matthew*, 3:326.

THE SHAPE OF MATTHEW'S STORY

Jewish War, 2.433–34, 444, 652; 6.313; 7.29–31). Jesus warns that *this is not the end* (vv. 6, 13). All will suffer from ongoing wars and tribulations (vv. 6–7, 15–22), including the Christian community (vv. 9, 10–12, 22). Once again, *this is not the end* (vv. 8). The eschatological end of all time lies in the future, and one who perseveres through trials and tribulations until that unknown time will be saved (v. 13). Between the current experiences of suffering, division, the destruction of Jerusalem, and the end of time: "the gospel of the kingdom will be preached throughout the world as a witness to all the nations."[8] Only then "the end will come" (v. 14), the final coming of the Son of Man as judge, accompanied by signs (v. 27). This moment will be as evident and inevitable as the gathering of vultures around a corpse (v. 28).

The End of the World: 24:29–35

The final coming of the Son of Man will be marked by the signs prophesied by Isaiah (24:29; Isa 13:10, 13), and the eschatological judgment (v. 30; see Dan 7:13–14). The angels will reach out to the four winds, the four corners of the heavens. They gather the elect from the nations, while "all the tribes of the earth will mourn" (vv. 30–31). The end-time has a double edge: the gathering of the elect and the despair of the sinful.

As they can read the signs of nature in the fruitfulness of the fig tree, the audience should read the signs of the advent of the Son of Man. Jesus promises that "this generation" will witness these events (v. 34). This puzzling promise, as we look back across two thousand years of Christian history, are words from Matthew to his audience. The early

---

8. Scholars debate whether Matthew includes or excludes Israel among the "nations." See the summary, supporting the inclusive interpretation in Francis J. Moloney, *The Resurrection of the Messiah: A Narrative Commentary on the Resurrection Accounts in the Four Gospels* (New York: Paulist Press, 2013), 53–54, 66n70.

The Messiah's Death and Resurrection in Jerusalem

Church strongly believed in the imminent return of Jesus as the judge of humankind (see, e.g., 1 Thess 4:13–18; 1 Cor 7:25–31; Mark 9:1). Matthew asks his audience to share his belief that the end-time is not "now," but near at hand. Matthew's timing may have been wrong (see his awareness of that in v. 36), but the promise of a final coming of the Son of Man as judge remains firm. These words of Jesus "will not pass away" (v. 35).

THE NEED FOR WATCHFULNESS: 24:36 – 25:30

A period will elapse between the dramatic destruction of Jerusalem and its temple, accompanied by suffering and division, and the end of all time. Jesus addresses the watchful behavior required of those whose perseverance throughout the in-between-time will lead to salvation (see v. 13).

The Unknown Day and Hour: 24:36–44

Counterbalancing Jesus' words in verse 34, only the Father knows and will determine the end-time (v. 36). An example from Israel's Scriptures and two examples from day-to-day life exemplify this truth. In the days of Noah, life went on, until the flood brought destruction on the unwary revelers. So will it be "at the coming of the Son of Man" (vv. 36–39). Two men or two women might be about their task; one will be taken and the other left. No one knows why or whom. No one knows the hour; all must "stay awake" (vv. 40–42). A master of a house does not know when his house may be broken into by a thief. If he did, he would "stay awake" (v. 43).

The Greek verb translated "stay awake" in verses 42 and 43 (*grēgoreō*) does not mean "keep one's eyes open." It summons faithfulness to duties and responsibilities (see 26:38, 40, 41). Because of the unknown hour of the coming of the Son of Man, Matthew's audience is exhorted to be prepared (v. 44). The parables that follow (the faithful or unfaithful servant [24:45-51], the ten virgins [25:1-13], and the talents [vv. 14-30]) drive home that exhortation. They urge a Christian audience "to stay awake" in the time between the presence of Jesus of Nazareth and the final coming of the Son of Man (see 25:13: *grēgoreite*).

The Faithful or Unfaithful Servant: 24:45-51

Who is the "faithful and prudent servant" (v. 45)? The one who says nothing but does his duty (v. 46), or the one who promises much but does nothing (vv. 48-49)? The parousia is inevitable. The sudden arrival of the master ("on an unexpected day" [v. 50]) leads to blessing and reward for the former (the one who does his or her duty), and condemnation and punishment for the latter (vv. 50-51). The parousia is inevitable.

The Ten Bridesmaids: 25:1-13

Matthew adopts a wedding setting to indicate the unknown time of the arrival of the eschatological bridegroom (see 9:15; 22:1-10; 24:36-44), the blessing of those who are "faithful and prudent" (25:10; see 24:45), and the exclusion of those who are not (vv. 11-12). Whatever the delay might be, Matthew insists that his audience "stay awake" (*grēgoreite*) (v. 13; see 24:42, 43).

The Talents: 25:14-30

The Greek word *talanton* does not mean "talent" but a measure of weight, a very large unit of wealth. The master has gone but will come back "after a long time" (v. 19; see 24:8; 25:5). How is one to behave during this time? Those servants who have profited from the major financial trust the master placed in them over a long period of time (vv. 16–17) are blessed, sharing in the master's joy (vv. 20–23). The one who has done nothing with that trust, knowing the exacting nature of the master and his dealings with his servants (vv. 24–25), is condemned (vv. 26–28, 30). He has spent the time of the master's absence as a "wicked, lazy servant," the exact opposite of watching, faithful, and prudent servant (v. 26).

The eschatological nature of the master's response is highlighted by the promise that the blessed share his master's joy (vv. 21, 23), while the punishment meted out to the one who failed is the loss of anything he had (v. 29), and his being cast out into "the darkness outside" (v. 30). A veiled attack on the leaders of Israel, recipients of God's promises who have not attended to them, may lie behind Jesus' words: "even what he has will be taken away" (v. 29).

THE JUDGMENT OF THE NATIONS: 25:31–46

Matthew closes this section of his story with the only New Testament description of the end-time. The scene is set through a second description of the coming of the Son of Man, accompanied by his angels and the gathering of the nations "when the Son of Man comes in his glory" (v. 31–32a.; see 16:27; 19:28; 24:39–41). He will act as a shepherd (see 2:6; 9:36; 18:12; 26:31), separating the sheep from the goats (v. 32b–33; see Ezek 34:17–19).

The enthroned Son of Man, now described as "the king" declares the sheep on his right "blessed by my Father." They "inherit the kingdom" prepared for them "from the foundation of the world" (v. 34). The reason for their blessedness is their care for Jesus Christ when he was hungry, thirsty, a stranger, naked, ill, and imprisoned (vv. 35–36). Unaware when they have behaved in this way, the Son of Man informs them that they cared for others, for "the least brethren of mine," the fragile in the community (vv. 37–40). The goats on the left are sent away "into the eternal fire prepared for the devil and his angels" (v. 41). They did not care for others (vv. 41–45): "What you did not do for one of these least ones, you did not do it for me" (v. 45). Judgment follows: the wicked to eternal punishment and the righteous to eternal life (v. 46).

Matthew's description of the final judgment does not come as a surprise to his audience. The expression "little ones" has been used to refer to the community, those who follow the self-sacrificing way of Jesus Christ. In his Sermon on the Mount Jesus called his disciples to the perfection of love, for one another and for one's enemies (5:43–48). At the heart of the same discourse, as he taught them how to pray (6:9–13), he described consequences of such prayer: "If you forgive others their transgressions, your heavenly Father will forgive you. But if you do not forgive others, neither will your Father forgive your transgressions" (vv. 14–15). As he closed this sermon, he summarized its message: "Do to others whatever you would have them do to you. This is the law and the prophets" (7:12; see 5:17–20).

Later, Jesus exhorts his audience "to become like little children" (18:1–5), and he issues stern warnings to those who cause "the little ones" to stumble and fall (18:6–14). Questioned on the greatest commandment, Jesus responds, "You shall love the Lord your God with all your heart, with all your soul, and all your mind. This is the greatest and first commandment. The second is like it: You shall love your neighbor as yourself. The whole law and the prophets depend on these commandments" (22:37–40). God wants mercy, not sacrifice (9:13; 12:7; see Hos 6:6). The final judgment that Jesus describes will not be measured by human achievement, but by mercy for the suffering. "The whole law and the prophets depend on these commandments" (22:40).

The Messiah's Death and Resurrection in Jerusalem

Jesus' ministry closes with a focus on "endings." The end of Jerusalem is not the end of all time (24:4-28). But that time will come, as the Son of Man, accompanied by signs, will come as judge (24:29-35). Between "now" and "the end-time" vigilance is required (24:26–25:30). At the final judgment the king will separate the sheep and the goats according to their care for the suffering "little ones" (25:31-46).

JESUS' PASSION, DEATH, AND RESURRECTION: MATTHEW 26:1 – 28:15

Matthew's passion narrative depends on his source, Mark 14:1–15:47. Jesus interacts with his disciples and Jewish authorities at the final supper and the Jewish hearing (26:1-75); then with Roman authority and other characters at the Roman hearing and the crucifixion (27:1-71). The following scheme shows that this is the case, using *italics* to highlight Matthew's additions, and alterations of Mark's original.

The Shape of Matthew 26:1-75: Jesus, His Disciples, and the Jewish Hearing

26:1-2: *Matthean introduction*: a fourth passion prediction
    [A] 26:3-5: The plot of the Jewish leaders
        [B] vv. 6-13: The anointing of Jesus
    [A] vv. 14-16: Judas, *one of the Twelve*, joins the plot
        [B] vv. 17-19: Jesus prepares for a Passover meal
    [A] vv. 20-25: Jesus predicts the betrayal of Judas. Matthew has Judas ask if he is the betrayer, and Jesus affirms that he is the one (v. 25).

THE SHAPE OF MATTHEW'S STORY

[B] vv. 26-30: Jesus shares the meal with his disciples. Matthew adds in Jesus' words over the cup: "for the forgiveness of sins" (v. 28).
[A] vv. 31-35: Jesus predicts the denials of Peter and the flight of the disciples.
[B] vv. 36-46: The prayer of Jesus in Gethsemane
[A] vv. 47-56: The betrayal of Judas and the flight of the disciples. Matthew has Jesus address Judas as "friend," and asks why he is there (v. 50). Only Matthew has Jesus telling Peter to put away his sword, indicating that he could ask God for help, but that this must happen to fulfill the Scriptures (vv. 52-54).
[B] vv. 57-68: Jesus reveals his identity at the Jewish trial.
[A] vv. 69-75: Peter denies Jesus three times. *Matthew adds the comment: "Then Peter remembered the word that Jesus had spoken: 'Before the cock crows, you will deny me three times.' He went outside and began to weep bitterly"* (v. 75).

The first part of Jesus' passion is deliberately shaped by intercalating positive and negative moments in the story. It is introduced by Matthew's use of a final passion prediction in 26:1-2 that does not mention the resurrection. This prediction marks the end of Jesus' ministry and his acceptance of what lies ahead. Across eleven scenes, six of them are negative [A]. One of the Twelve joins the plot of the Jewish leaders and agrees to betray him (26:3-5, 14-16); Jesus predicts that Judas will betray him (vv. 20-25); Jesus predicts that Peter will deny him, and all the disciples will flee (vv. 31-35). The betrayal takes place (vv. 47-56). The denial and the flight take place (vv. 69-75). This tragedy is accompanied by Jesus' gestures of love and self-revelation across five scenes [B]: the anointing in preparation for burial (vv.

The Messiah's Death and Resurrection in Jerusalem

6-13); Jesus' preparation for a final meal with his disciples (vv. 17-19), and Jesus shares a meal with them (vv. 26-30). Jesus demonstrates unconditional obedience to the Father (vv. 36-46), and he reveals himself as the Christ, the Son of God, and the Son of Man at the Jewish trial (vv. 57-68).

Flanked by prophecies of betrayal (vv. 20-25: fifth scene), denial and flight (vv. 31-35: seventh scene), in the central sixth scene Jesus breaks bread and shares wine with his disciples. Only in the First Gospel Jesus teaches that the covenant sealed by the sharing of the cup is "for the forgiveness of sins" (v. 28; see Jer 31:34; Exod 24:8). Matthew continues to tell a story of understanding, love, forgiveness, and compassion.

In his prophecy of Judas' betrayal, Jesus indicates that he is already aware of his identity (v. 25), and in the event of the betrayal, as well as the kiss (see Mark 14:45; Matt 26:49), he addresses Judas as "friend," and asks why he finds himself in that situation (v. 50). He tells Peter and the disciples that there is no call for a sword, as "it must come to pass in this way"…that "the scriptures be fulfilled" (vv. 52-54); "that the writings of the prophets may be fulfilled" (v. 56). Most poignantly, the juxtaposition of the weeping of Peter and the despair and suicide of Judas, who has been called "friend" to the last, indicates two alternatives to the rejection of Jesus that no doubt spoke to the readers and hearers of this dramatic account. Sorrow and repentance bring forgiveness; despair and loss of all hope produces a senseless suicide (vv. 26:75; 27:3-10).

> Matthew shapes the traditional account of Jesus' last night with his disciples and the Jewish hearing around a series of intercalations that deny or affirm the Christology of the

THE SHAPE OF MATTHEW'S STORY

story. At the center of 26:1-75 Jesus shares a meal with his fragile disciples "for the forgiveness of sins" (vv. 26-30).

Although briefer, Matthew's account of Jesus' execution as the crucifixion of the King also continues this staged presentation of scenes that alternate across positive and negative intercalations.

The Shape of Matthew 27:1-61: Jesus, the Roman Trial, and Crucifixion

[B] 27:1-14: Jesus reveals himself as King to the Roman authority.

[A] vv. 15-23: The question of Barabbas, and the choice of a false messianic hope. Matthew adds *the intervention of Pilate's wife, asking that he have nothing to do with this righteous man* (v. 19).

[B] vv. 24-26: Pilate proclaims *Jesus innocent* and *King*. Matthew adds *Pilate's washing of his hands, claiming innocence in the face of turbulence, and the terrible cry of "the whole people": "His blood be upon us and upon our children"* (vv. 24-25).

[A] vv. 27-31: The Roman soldiers mock Jesus (King!).

[B] vv. 32-37: The crucifixion of "the King of the Jews"

[A] vv. 37-44: The crucified is mocked (King, Son of God, and Savior).

[B] vv. 45-54: The death of Jesus. Matthew inserts a description *of apocalyptic signs that accompany Jesus' death* (27:51-54).

[A] vv. 55-56: The women at the cross.

[B] vv. 57-61: Burial of Jesus, watched by the women.

The Messiah's Death and Resurrection in Jerusalem

Matching the literary and theological structure of 26:1–75, in verses 32–37 the fifth of nine scenes, the central episode, Matthew reports the death of Jesus without any direct speech (vv. 32–37). It closes with the title on the cross: "This is Jesus, the King of the Jews" (v. 37). Like the centerpiece of Jesus' final presence with failing disciples (26:25–35), his death is surrounded by scenes of parallel failure. In the fourth scene, the Roman soldiers abuse Jesus and ironically announce the truth that he is "King of the Jews" (vv. 27–31). In the sixth scene, passersby and the Jewish leaders abuse him, ironically proclaim him as God's Son, Savior, and King of Israel (vv. 38–44). Set between this ironic use of abuse by all who surround him to proclaim the truth, the wordless crucifixion scene (vv. 32–37) is the grim enthronement of the Son of God, the King of Israel, the Savior.

Matthew eases Pilate's responsibility for the death of Jesus (the intervention of his wife, and his handwashing), and locates the Jewish leaders, and eventually "the whole people," as the driving force for the crucifixion of the innocent King of Israel, Son of God, and Savior. Opposition to Jesus from the leaders of Israel has steadily increased (11:2—16:12 [tension]; 16:13—20:34 [public antagonism]). It now reaches its tragic climax.

At the Roman trial, "the whole people" join the rejection of Jesus in their cry that his blood be upon them, and upon their children (27:24–25). This cry from the Jewish people was never uttered. Written for a Christian community that has left its home in the synagogue, Matthew uses his story of Jesus to show that Jesus fulfilled Israel's Sacred Scriptures in his mission to "the lost sheep of Israel." He is the perfect continuation of God's design for the true Israel. However, the leaders of Israel rejected Jesus and the Christian community, the ongoing presence of Jesus (see 1:23; 28:20).

THE SHAPE OF MATTHEW'S STORY

Matthew reports events, using the imagery of Jewish apocalyptic texts, immediately following the death of Jesus.

> From noon onward, darkness came over the whole land until three in the afternoon.…And behold, the veil of the sanctuary was torn in two from top to bottom. The earth quaked, rocks were split, tombs were opened, and the bodies of many saints who had fallen asleep were raised. And coming forth from their tombs after his resurrection, they entered the holy city and appeared to many. (27:45, 51–54)

Not only the centurion (as in Mark 15:39), but also those keeping watch with him (vv. 35–36: Roman soldiers) "saw the earthquake and all that was happening, and they said, 'Truly, this was the Son of God!'" (v. 54).

The collection of apocalyptic phenomena that accompany Jesus' death and leads to the confession of the centurion and all those present, is found only in the First Gospel. Matthew has drawn upon apocalyptic symbols from Jewish tradition, but he has *shifted their timing*. The events described—darkening of the skies, splitting of the rocks, and the rising of the dead—are events that were expected at the end of time when God would return as Lord and Judge (see Amos 8:9; Joel 2:10; Hag 2:6; Zech 14:5; Dan 12:2; Jer 15:9; Ezek 37:7, 12–13; Isa 26:19; Dan 12:2). Matthew indicates that these events will take place *not only* at the end of all history, as was held by Jewish tradition, and also by Matthew (see 24:29–31; 25:31–32). They have *already happened* at the death of Jesus. Heaven and earth are passing away (see 5:18).

The Messiah's Death and Resurrection in Jerusalem

THE AFTERMATH OF JESUS' DEATH: 27:62—28:20

The holy ones who rise from their open graves go into the city "after his resurrection." Matthew announces, as Jesus dies, that he will rise (v. 53). He continues to follow Mark's description of the aftermath of Jesus' death: the presence of the woman at the cross, the burial by Joseph of Arimathea, watched by women. But he perseveres in an alternation between negative and positive episodes.

> **The Shape of Matthew 27:62—28:20: The Resurrection and Appearances of Jesus**
>
> [A] 27:62-66: Negative: The setting of the guard at the tomb.
> [B] 28:1-10: Positive: The resurrection of Jesus.
> [A] 28:11-15: Negative: The report of the guard to the Jewish authorities.
> [B] 28:16-20: Positive: The risen Jesus' final commission.

Repeating his practice of creating "bridge episodes" (see 16:13-23), in 27:62-66 Matthew reports the request of the Pharisees that a guard be set at the tomb. As one moment in the story closes (26:1—27:66), another opens (27:62—28:20).

Setting the Guard: 27:62-66

The leaders of Israel, the chief priests, and the Pharisees, ask Pilate to guard the tomb. They call Jesus an "imposter,"

THE SHAPE OF MATTHEW'S STORY

recalling his predictions that he would rise again on the third day (vv. 62–63; see 16:21; 17:22–23; 20:17–19). They must put a stop to fraudulent behavior on the part of any of his disciples, who might steal the body and then tell the people that "he has been raised from the dead" (v. 64). Pilate allows them to have the guard of soldiers, but the Jewish leadership sees to it that the tomb is made secure (v. 65). They seal the sepulcher with a stone and set a guard (v. 66).

The Resurrection of Jesus: 28:1–10

Matthew provides the only attempt in the New Testament to describe events that surrounded the resurrection of Jesus. He focuses on the fact that it takes place "after the Sabbath, as the first day of the week was dawning," Matthew names the women journeying to the tomb "Mary Magdalene and the other Mary" (v. 1; see 27:61). They experience events that recall the apocalyptic language used at Jesus' death in 27:51–54.

> And behold, there was a great earthquake; for an angel of the Lord descended from heaven, approached, rolled back the stone, and sat upon it. His appearance was like lightning, and his clothing was white as snow. The guards were shaken with fear of him and became like dead men (28:2–4).

Reporting events traditionally associated with predictions of the end of all time, Matthew points to the death and resurrection of Jesus as the turning point of the ages (see 5:17–20). God will not only enter human history at the end of time; he has anticipated that entry in Jesus' death and resurrection. Time and the events of humankind will continue as history unfolds, but Jesus' death and resurrection transform everything.

The Messiah's Death and Resurrection in Jerusalem

The angelic figure at the tomb takes on the role of a heavenly messenger. The women knew Jesus of Nazareth, and they have seen him crucified (27:55–56). He has been raised, as he had said (16:21; 17:22–23; 20:17–19). The women are to look at the place where those who killed him allowed him to be buried (28:6). The angel commissions them to go quickly to the disciples and announce that he has been raised from the dead and is going ahead of them to Galilee (v. 7), as he promised at the supper (26:32). The angel repeats Jesus' earlier words, instructing them to go into Galilee (see 26:32). They depart from the tomb "with fear." The women may be afraid, but they are "overjoyed." They are to become the first to announce the Easter message (Matt 28:8).

On their way to announce the message, the risen Jesus met them, greeting them with a salutation that catches the joy that marked their departure from the tomb: "Rejoice" (v. 9). Their response is that of a respectful "going to him." Matthew uses one of his favorite verbs to report the women's approach to Jesus (*proserchomai*). It has appeared across the story to tell of the approach of the sick or other petitioners who seek Jesus (see 8:2, 5, 19, 25; 9:14, 20, 28; 13:10, 36; 15:30; 17:14; 18:21; 19:16; 20:20; 21:14; 26:7). Their approach leads to an affectionate taking hold of his feet and a humble bowing down before him. The Greek verb used to indicate their bowing down (*proskuneō*) is another of Matthew's favorite words to indicate recognition of the presence of the divine in Jesus' story (see 2:2, 8, 11; 4:9, 10; 8:2; 9:18; 14:33; 15:25; 20:20; 28:17).

In 27:7, the angel sent the women to announce the Easter message to "the disciples." Jesus adds to the message. They are to go to "my brothers" (28:10). Because of the transforming events of Jesus' death and resurrection, the recipients of the Easter message are no longer "disciples," but "brothers."

The Report of the Guard to the Jewish Authorities: 28:11-15

As the women make their way to announce the resurrection to the disciples, some of the guard from 27:61-66 is on its way to the chief priests. They, like the women, will also tell "all that had happened" (v. 11). One report is a lie (vv. 13-14) and the other the truth (vv. 7-8). As Judas was led astray with the promise of money (26:14-16), so are the soldiers (28:12). They are to tell a lie: "His disciples came by night and stole him while we were asleep" (v. 13). The result of the soldiers' accepting the money and telling the story of the stolen body leads to the point of this final negative report: "This story has circulated among the Jews to this day" (v. 15). The Matthean community tells the story of the resurrection of Jesus, and his appearances; the Jews tell the story of a body stolen by his disciples. The audience must decide which story they live by.

CHAPTER SEVEN

The Great Commission
Matthew 28:16–20

The final scene in the First Gospel is a key to its interpretation. "All of the basic theological statements of the Gospel of Matthew seem to be gathered up in these forty words at the end of the Gospel."[1] Matthew 28:16–20 leads the audience into the "the time of the church" (see Matt 16:18; 18:17). Eleven disciples (as Judas has left the Twelve in despair [27:3-10]) went into Galilee, to the mountain, instructed by Jesus to meet him there (28:16). This is not the first time Jesus has summoned his disciples to the top of a mountain to give them important instructions (see 4:8–9; 5:1–2; 7:28–29; 17:6–7). On a final mountain in Galilee, some worship him, "but they doubted" (28:17).

Jesus opens his final instructions with a declaration about himself, and then spells out the consequences of such a declaration for his disciples and their mission. All authority in heaven and on earth has been given to him (v. 18). Jesus, who had been crucified, is now exalted to power and authority over all creation. Jesus claims the authority that Israel allowed only to Yhwh (see Deut 6:4–9; Dan 7:14). Based on that claim, Jesus commissions his disciples.

---

1. Luz, *Matthew*, 3:621.

THE SHAPE OF MATTHEW'S STORY

1. He commands them: "Go, therefore, and make disciples of all nations" (v. 19a). They are to make "disciples." Matthew is almost the only New Testament author to use the verb "make disciples" (see 13:52; 27:57; see also, only Acts 14:21). He is also the evangelist who most frequently calls Jesus' disciples by the Greek expression for "disciple" (*mathētēs*). It means "one who learns from another." The eleven are "disciples," learning from Jesus. They are now to draw others into a community that learns from Jesus.
2. There was openness to the idea of a universal salvation in the prophets (see, e.g., Isa 2:1–4). It meant a movement from the Gentile world toward Sion. There is only one people of God, with its father Abraham, and its Law from Moses. This is transformed. A new people of God, founded by Jesus of Nazareth, are to "go out" to make disciples of all nations.[2]
3. The disciples are further instructed to "baptize" in the name of the Father and of the Son and of the Holy Spirit (v. 19b). Jesus institutes a new initiation rite. The risen Jesus asks that baptism replace the initiation rite of circumcision. At Jesus' baptism the voice of the Father came from heaven and the Spirit of God descended on Jesus (3:16–17). The new initiation ritual: "On the one hand…expresses the belonging that is constitutive of the baptized persons, on the other hand…reminds them of the baptism itself in which these three names were 'proclaimed' over the person who was being baptized."[3]
4. The final command broadens the source of traditional Jewish faith. Jesus uses words commonly found in

---

2. On "the nations," see above, p. 98, note 8.
3. Luz, *Matthew*, 3:632.

The Great Commission

passages on the importance of the Torah: "to teach," "to observe," "to command" (see, e.g., Deut 5—6, especially 6:1, where all these terms appear). But he provides a new teaching: "teaching them to observe all that I have commanded you" (v. 20a). The Law of Moses has been perfected in the teaching of Jesus (5:17-20), but Jesus does not instruct his disciples to abandon the Law and replace it with the teaching of Jesus. The Law will be interpreted through the teaching of Jesus. The teaching of the disciples is found in discourses of Matthew's story of Jesus: on the ethical organization of the community (5:1—7:29), the mission and lifestyle of the disciples (10:1-42), the nature of the kingdom (13:1-52), the quality of life and care in the community (18:1-35), and on the end of time and the purpose of history (24:1—25:46).

Jesus' final words are not ones of departure, but an assurance that he will always be with his disciples (v. 20b). These words point back to 1:23, where Jesus was announced as the Emmanuel, "God with us." The theme of the presence of Jesus has sounded across the entire story (see 9:15; 17:17; 18:20), with special intensity in the passion narrative (26:11, 18, 20, 23, 29, 36, 38, 40, 51, 69, 71). There are repeated stories of Jesus' helping presence among his disciples (see 8:23-27; 14:13-21, 22-23; 15:29-39; 17:1-8; 26:26-29).

Although Matthew's story ends here, between Jesus' death and resurrection and his return as the Son of Man there will be persecution when many will fall away (13:21). There will be a mixture of good and bad in the Church (13:24-30). Many will grow weary waiting for his return (25:1-13), but at the end of the age Jesus will come as the Son of Man to judge the nations (25:31-46).

THE SHAPE OF MATTHEW'S STORY

The final commission (28:16-20) is not an ending, but a beginning that invites the audience to discipleship and to the evangelization of the nations in the period between the death and resurrection of Jesus, the turning point of the ages (5:17-18; 27:45, 51-53; 28:2-3), and the final coming of the Son of Man (24:29-31; 25:31-46).

Epilogue

Meticulous Matthew

PROLOGUE

A prologue (Matt 1:1 — 4:16) introduces "the book of the genealogy of Jesus Christ, the Son of God, the Son of Abraham" (1:1). Matthew establishes the truth of these claims across 1:1 — 4:16. The infancy story presents who Jesus is and where he is from (1:18 — 2:23). The witness of the Baptist and the baptism of Jesus (3:1-17), the testing of God's Son (4:1-11), and his withdrawal to Galilee of the nations (vv. 12-16) leaves the audience in no doubt about the identity and the mission of Jesus. But only the audience possesses this "inside information."

MINISTRY OF WORD AND DEED IN GALILEE

A new stage of the narrative begins in 4:17: "From that time on, Jesus began to preach" (4:17). Jesus teaches and heals across 5:1 — 9:34, clamped between the summaries of 4:23 and 9:35: "He went around all of Galilee, teaching in their synagogues, proclaiming the gospel of the kingdom, and curing every disease and illness among the people"

(4:23; see 9:35). He opened this part of his story with the call of his first disciples (4:18–22). He closes it with their association with Jesus' mission (10:1–42). In 11:1, Matthew signs off on Jesus' initial mission in Galilee: "When Jesus finished giving these commands to his twelve disciples, he went away from that place to teach and to preach in their towns."

A CRISIS EMERGES

A new chord is struck as Matthew focuses on two sides of a growing tension across 11:2 — 16:23. On the one hand, the mission and identity of Jesus is uncovered; a "new family" gathers around him. On the other, opposition and animosity mounts. To convey this, Matthew shapes his narrative around three episodes. In an opening episode, John the Baptist asks if Jesus is the expected Messiah (11:1-19; see v. 3). His execution is reported in 14:1–12. Matthew 11:2 — 16:23 closes with Peter's response to John's question, along with his hesitancy, at Caesarea Philippi (16:13-23). Between the accounts of the query and death of the Baptist (11:2–19; 14:1-12). Matthew draws his audience into the story. The literary intercalation of accounts that report Jesus' rejection (11:20-24; 12:1-14, 22-37, 43-45; 13:54-58) and affirmation (11:25-30; 12:15-21, 38-42, 46-50) generates a call to decision. Within these intercalations, Jesus delivers his parable discourse, an interlude that blesses those who are granted access the kingdom, condemning those who do not (13:1-53). This steady presentation of rejection and affirmation asks an audience who has experienced the prologue (1:1 — 4:16), whose side are you on? Are you "in" or "out" (13:1-53; see vv. 10–17)?

The second moment in this literary unit is shaped by two feeding miracles and their consequences. Set in Israel,

Epilogue

the first feeding miracle (14:13-21) leads to Jesus' interaction with his disciples (14:22-33; 15:15-20) and an explicit rejection of the man-made traditions of Israel (15:1-14). He turns to the Gentile world (15:21-31) and provides nourishment (15:32-39). Jesus again deals with his rejection by the leaders of Israel (16:1-4), and the "little faith" of the disciples (16:5-12). Peter enacts that "little faith" at Caesarea Philippi. He makes a full-blooded confession of faith (16:13-20) but rejects the way of the Son of Man (16:13-23). Unlike John the Baptist (14:1-12), he is not able to put his life where his words are. Like the leaders of Israel (see 15:1-14), Peter is thinking "as human beings do" (16:23).

THE JOURNEY TO JERUSALEM

The account of the journey to Jerusalem is framed by the confession of Peter in 16:13-20 and the confession of the blind men in 20:29-34. It features three passion predictions (16:21-23; 17:22-23; 20:17-23). Peter, the disciples, and the sons of Zebedee fail to accept or understand Jesus' predictions. After the first (16:21-23), disciples are called to follow Jesus to the cross (16:24-28). God's beloved Son calls them (17:1-13), and they need oneness with God in prayer (vv. 14-20). After the second (17:22-23), lengthy consideration is given to the challenges of living as a follower of Jesus in the "real world." Framed by two affirmations of the sovereignty of God (17:24-27; 20:1-16), Jesus instructs the disciples on receptivity (18:1-9; 19:13-15), forgiveness (18:10-35), marriage (19:1-12), and possessions (19:16-30). His teaching turns the world upside down: "For human beings this is impossible, but for God all things are possible" (19:26). After the third prediction (20:17-23), Jesus instructs on the cross (20:20-23) and service (vv. 24-27). He points to himself as the Son of Man who is not served, but who serves, and gives his life for the ransom of many (20:28). The section closes as blind men at Jericho confess their faith (see 16:13–20), despite opposition (vv. 29–34). They are models for all disciples: "They received their sight and followed him" (v. 34).

JESUS IN JERUSALEM

The story of Jesus' presence in Jerusalem is shaped by his movements. *He enters the city* (21:1–11) and brings all cultic activity in the temple to a standstill (vv. 12–22). A series of other "endings" follow. After a series of parables that punish the leaders of Israel (21:23—22:14), he argues with the Pharisees, the Sadducees, and debates issues of the Law and the Scriptures. He reduces everyone to silence (22:15–46). He condemns the hypocrisy of the Scribes and the Pharisees in a way that questions all established religions (23:1–39).

He leaves the temple and the city. Looking back from the Mount of Olives, Jesus predicts the end of Jerusalem, and the end of the world (24:1–35). Time must elapse between these two "endings" so that "the gospel of the kingdom will be preached throughout the world" (24:14). Watchfulness must mark that period (24:36—25:30), until the Son of Man comes as king to separate the sheep from the goats (25:31–46).

Jesus predicts his death, (26:1–2), and once more *in the city* (vv. 17–19) Matthew adopts meticulously arranged positive and negative intercalations to tell the traditional story of the passion, death, and resurrection of Jesus. The account of Jesus, his disciples, and the Jewish hearings is formed by eleven such episodes (26:3–75). The centerpiece (vv. 26:30: the sixth episode) tells of Jesus breaking bread and shar-

Epilogue

ing wine with his fragile disciples "for the forgiveness of sins" (v. 28). The account of Jesus, the Roman trial and the crucifixion, is told through nine alternating intercalations. The fifth episode (vv. 32–37) reports the crucifixion of the King of the Jews. The women at the cross (vv. 55–56), watching the burial of Jesus (vv. 57–61), form a "bridge" from the events at the cross into those surrounding his resurrection.

THE RESURRECTION AND APPEARANCES OF JESUS

Intercalation continues, culminating in Jesus' final commission of the eleven on the mountain in Galilee (27:62 – 28:20). As the story began in Galilee with a promise that God is "with us" in Jesus (1:23), it closes in the same location, with the same promise: "I am with you always, until the end of the age" (28:20).

CONCLUSION

A scribe trained for the kingdom (13:52), Matthew has used his skills to draw people into the new family of Jesus, believers who do the will of the Father in heaven (12:49–50). He has worked meticulously with traditions of his own, others from Mark and some he shares with Luke (Q). Nothing is left to chance.[1] He has used numerous techniques to give shape to his story: inclusions, chiasms, framed narratives, intercalations, bridge episodes, and triads.

He has had regular recourse to series of intercalated

---

1. The expression "meticulous Matthew" was widely used by Peter F. Ellis, *Matthew: His Mind and His Message* (Collegeville: Liturgical Press, 1973).

THE SHAPE OF MATTHEW'S STORY

presentations of the positive and negative responses to the presence and teaching of Jesus during the developing crisis between Jesus and the leaders of Israel (11:2–14:12) and in the account of Jesus' death and resurrection (26:1-75; 27:1-61; 27:57–28:20). Parallel, although not identical, series of alternations follow the feeding miracles (14:22–15:31; 16:1-23) and return in Jesus' systematic encounter with the institutions of Israel (21:23–23:39). Matthew has informed his audience who Jesus was, and what he has done for humankind in his prologue (1:1–4:16). His sustained use of literary intercalations across the story invites his audience to accept that the crucified and risen Jesus the Nazarene is indeed the Messiah, the Son of David, the Son of Abraham, born of the Spirit, the King of Israel, "Jesus," who will save his people from their sins, "God with us," who lives by every word that comes from the mouth of God (1:1–4:16; see 4:4). Matthew's meticulous story asks: Whose side are you on?

Appendix One

The Shape of Matthew's Story

Matthew has used several literary techniques to shape his story. The following synthesis of the "shape" of the story summarizes how it affects the story's internal development and movement from one stage to another. A schematic "outline" of Matthew's story is provided in a final appendix.

I. *1:1 – 4:16*. The prologue begins with a christological presentation of Jesus as the Christ, the son of David and the son of Abraham (1:1). As well as being the fulfillment of Jewish messianic hopes, he is the son of Abraham, the father of all nations (see Gen 12:1-3; 22:18), the Son of God (3:16-17; 4:1-11). Gentiles play an important role: Gentile women in the genealogy (1:1-17), and the coming of the wise men from the east (2:1-12). The prologue closes with the presentation of Jesus in Galilee of the Gentiles, a light to those who dwelt in darkness (4:15-16). An inclusion (see 1:1 and 4:15-16) sets the limits of the passage.

II. *4:17 – 11:1*. Jesus' preaching (5:1 – 8:1a) and miraculous ministry (8:1b – 11:1) are set between two summaries (4:23; 9:35) delivered to disciples (4:17-25; 9:35-38). Matthew encloses his sermon on mission (10:5 – 10:42) between passages directed explicitly to the Twelve (10:1-4; 11:1a). A double inclusion (see 4:17-25 and 9:35-38 and 10:1-4 and 11:1a) sets the limits of the passage.

THE SHAPE OF MATTHEW'S STORY

III. *11:2 – 14:12*. The gradual intensification of hostility between Jesus and the leaders of Israel opens with the christological question of the Baptist from prison and Jesus' explanation of his role (11:2-19). It closes with the account of the Baptist's death (14:1-12). The mounting tension emerges through a series of eight intercalated episodes that alternate between Jesus' rejection and affirmation (11:20-24, 25-30; 12:1-14, 15-21, 22-37, 38-42, 43-45, 46-50; 13:54-58; 14:1-12). Into these intercalations, Matthew inserts the parable discourse explaining the difference between those who belong or do not belong to the kingdom (13:1-53).

IV. *14:13 – 16:23*. The pattern of inclusion is replaced by two feeding miracles, one in Israel (14:13-21) and the other among the Gentiles (15:32-39), followed by a fourfold series of matching incidents revealing the failure of the leaders of Israel and the little faith of the disciples and Peter (14:22-31; 16:1-23). Matthew introduces a "bridge episode." Peter's encounter with Jesus at Caesarea Philippi closes 14:13 – 16:23. His confession of faith (16:13-20) and his failure to accept Jesus' destiny in Jerusalem (vv. 21-23) also introduce the journey to Jerusalem (16:13 – 20:34): "From that time on Jesus began to show his disciples that he must go to Jerusalem" (16:21).

V. *16:13 – 20:34*. The confession of Peter (16:13-20) and the confession of the blind men at Jericho (20:29-34) form an inclusion that sets the limits of the narrative of Jesus' journey to Jerusalem. Between the inclusion, Jesus predicts his death and resurrection three times (16:21-23; 17:22-23; 20:17-23). As each prediction is rejected or misunderstood by the disciples, Jesus instructs them on the nature of discipleship (16:24 – 17:20; 17:24 – 20:16; 20:22-28). The second (central) instruction (17:24 – 20:16) focusses on a radical reversal of accepted cultural norms (receptivity, forgive-

Appendix One

ness, marriage, and possessions). It is framed by an internal inclusion affirming the absolute sovereignty of God, with whom nothing is impossible (17:24-27; 20:1-16).

VI. *21:1 – 25:46*. Jesus' motion determines the shape of the account of his presence in Jerusalem. *He enters the city* (21:1-11). While there *he enters and exits the temple*, symbolically bringing its activities to an end (21:12-22). Between a further *entrance into the temple* (21:23) and a final *exit from the temple* (24:1), he criticizes the leaders of Israel (21:23 – 22:14), argues with them, reducing them to silence (22:15-46). He condemns them (23:1-39). *He leaves the city and its temple* (24:1) to deliver a discourse on the end of Jerusalem (24:1-28), the end of the world (24:29-35), and the need for watchfulness in the in-between-time (24:36 – 25:30).

VII. *26:1 – 28:20*. Jesus' final passion prediction (26:1-2) provides the theme for the climax of the narrative. Matthew leads the audience through a long intercalation of eleven negative and positive responses to Jesus on the part of the disciples and the leaders of Israel (26:3-75). The sixth (and central) passage reports Jesus' words and actions at a meal with his disciples, an anticipation of his self-gift "for the forgiveness of sins" (vv. 26-30; see v. 28). He employs the same technique to report the Roman trial, execution, and burial of Jesus through nine intercalated responses (27:1-61). The fifth (central) passage reports Jesus' crucifixion (vv. 32-37) where he is ironically proclaimed as "King of the Jews" (v. 37). The intercalations between negative and positive responses continue as the events surrounding Jesus' resurrection are reported, culminating with the climactic positive presentation of Jesus' commissioning his disciples on a mountain in Galilee (27:62 – 28:20).

Matthew's entire story unfolds between an inclusion. As it begins, Jesus is described "God with us" (1:23). It

THE SHAPE OF MATTHEW'S STORY

closes with the promise of the risen Jesus: "I am with you always until the end of the age" (28:20). Matthew's steady use of inclusions and intercalations asks all who experience his story to make up their minds about God, Jesus, the kingdom, discipleship (the Church), and a way of life that questions dominant cultural absolutes.

Appendix Two

An Outline of Matthew's Story

The coming of the Messiah: 1:1 – 4:16
    Where from and where to: 1:1 – 2:23
    Jesus' messianic status affirmed and tested: 3:1 – 4:16

Jesus' ministry of preaching and healing: 4:17 – 11:1
    The call of the disciples and the beginning of Jesus' Ministry: 4:17-25
    The sermon on the mount: 5:1 – 8:1a
    Miracles and discipleship: 8:1b – 11:1

The crisis in the ministry of the Messiah: 11:2 – 16:23
    Are you the one who is to come?: 11:2 – 14:12
        Literary frame: Jesus and John the Baptist: 11:2-19
            Negative response: Unrepentant towns: 11:20-24
            Positive presentation of Jesus: The Father and the Son: 11:25-30
            Negative response: Sabbath conflicts: 12:1-14
            Positive presentation of Jesus: The chosen Servant: 12:15-21
            Negative response: Jesus and Beelzebul: 12:22-37
            Positive presentation of Jesus: Jesus and the sign of Jonah: 12:38-42
            Negative response: Return of the unclean spirit: 12:43-45
            Positive presentation of Jesus: The criterion for the new family of Jesus: 12:46-50

THE SHAPE OF MATTHEW'S STORY

    The parable discourse punishes the leaders of Israel and blesses the disciples: 13:1–53
    Negative response: Rejection at Nazareth: 13:54–58
    Literary frame: Jesus and John the Baptist: 14:1–12
Feeding and failure: 14:13 – 16:23
    The first feeding miracle — in Israel: 14:13–21
    Consequences: Israel and Peter fail: 14:22 – 15:31
        Jesus on the stormy sea. Peter and the disciples show "little faith": 14:22–33
        Jesus questions the traditions of Israel: 15:1–14
        An ignorant Peter asks for clarification: 15:15–20
        Healing of a Canaanite woman: Gentiles praise the God of Israel: 15:21–32
    The second feeding miracle — among the Gentiles: 15:32–39
    Consequences: Israel, the disciples, and Peter fail: 16:1–23
        The Pharisees seek a sign: 16:1–4
        Crossing the sea, disciples of "little faith" discuss the meaning of Jesus' words: 16:5–12
        Peter confesses that Jesus is the Son of Man, the Son of God. He is blessed: 16:13–20
        Peter refuses to accept that the Messiah must suffer, die, and rise. He is cursed: 16:21–23

The Messiah's journey to Jerusalem: 16:13 – 20:34
    Literary frame: Confession of Peter at Caesarea Philippi: 16:13–20
    The first passion prediction and Peter's failure: 16:21–23
        Jesus' response: 16:24 – 17:20
            Instruction on the cross: 16:24–28
            The instruction of the transfiguration: 17:1–13
            The instruction of the of the epileptic boy: 17:14–20
    The second passion prediction and the disciples' failure: 17:22–23

Appendix Two

    Jesus' response: 17:24 — 20:16
        Opening frame: Instruction on the sovereignty of God: 17:24-27
        Instruction on receptivity and the kingdom: 18:1-9
        Instruction on the good shepherd and limitless forgiveness: 18:10-35
        Instruction on marriage: 19:1-12
        Instruction on receptivity and the kingdom: 19:13-15
        Instruction on possessions: 19:16-30
        Closing frame: Instruction on the sovereignty of God: 20:1-16
    The third passion prediction and the failure of the sons of Zebedee: 20:17-23
        Jesus' response: 20:22-28
            Instruction of the sons of Zebedee on suffering and service: 20:20-23
            Instruction of the remaining ten of the Twelve on the call to service: 20:24-27
            Christological motivation for suffering and service: 20:28
    Literary frame: Confession of the two blind men at Jericho: 20:29-34

The Messiah's death and resurrection in Jerusalem: 21:1 — 28:15
    Jesus' entry and ministry in Jerusalem: 21:1 — 25:46
        Jesus enters Jerusalem: 21:1-11
        Jesus enters and exits the temple: the cursed fig tree: 21:12-22
        Jesus in the temple: 21:23 — 23:39
            Parables that punish the leaders of Israel: 21:23 — 22:14
                The question of Jesus' authority: 21:23-27
                The parable of the two sons: 21:28-32
                The parable of the tenants: 21:33-46
                The parable of the wedding feast: 22:1-14

THE SHAPE OF MATTHEW'S STORY

    Conflicts with the leaders of Israel: 22:15–46
        Conflict with the Pharisees: 22:15–22
        Conflict with the Sadducees: 22:23–27
        The greatest commandment: 22:34–40
        David's son: 22:41–46
Jesus leaves the temple: his end-time discourse: 24:1 — 25:46
    The end of Jerusalem: 24:1–28
    The end of the world: 24:29–35
    The need for watchfulness: 24:36–44
    The parable of the faithful and unfaithful slave: 24:45–51
    The parable of the ten bridesmaids: 25:1–15
    The parable of the talents: 25:14–30
    The judgment of the nations: 25:31–46
Jesus' passion, death, and resurrection: 26:1 — 28:15
    Jesus, the disciples, and the Jewish hearing: 26:1–75
    Jesus, the Roman trial, and crucifixion: 27:1–61
    The resurrection and appearances of Jesus: 27:62 — 28:15

The great commission: 28:16–20

Select Bibliography

Blomberg, Craig L. *Matthew: An Exegetical and Theological Exposition of Holy Scripture*. The New American Commentary. Nashville, TN: Broadman Press, 1992.
Byrne, Brendan. *Lifting the Burden: Reading Matthew's Gospel in the Church Today*. Collegeville, MN: Liturgical Press, 2004.
———. "Matthew." In *The Paulist Biblical Commentary*, edited by José Enrique Aguilar Chiu, Richard J. Clifford, Carol J. Dempsey, et al, 900–971. Mahwah, NJ: Paulist Press, 2018.
Carter, Warren. *Matthew: Storyteller, Interpreter, Evangelist*. 2nd ed. Peabody, MA: Hendrickson, 2004.
Davies, W. D., and Dale C. Allison Jr. *The Gospel according to Saint Matthew*. 3 vols. International Critical Commentary. Edinburgh: T. & T. Clark, 1988–97.
Edwards, Richard A. *Matthew's Story of Jesus*. Philadelphia: Fortress, 1985.
Garland, David E. *Reading Matthew: A Literary and Theological Commentary on the First Gospel*. New York: Crossroad, 1993.
Kingsbury, Jack Dean. *Matthew as Story*. 2nd ed. Philadelphia: Fortress, 1988.
Luz, Ulrich. *Matthew*. 3 vols. Hermeneia. Minneapolis: Fortress, 2001–7.
Meier, John P. *Matthew*. New Testament Message 3. Wilmington, DE: Michael Glazier, 1980.
Schreiner, Patrick. *Matthew, Disciple and Scribe: The First Gospel and Its Portrait of Jesus*. Grand Rapids: Baker Academic, 2019.
Schweizer, Eduard. *The Good News according to Matthew*. Translated by David E. Green. London: SPCK, 1975.

THE SHAPE OF MATTHEW'S STORY

Senior, Donald. *The Gospel of Matthew*. Interpreting Biblical Texts. Nashville, TN: Abingdon Press, 1997.

———. *Matthew*. Abingdon New Testament Commentaries. Nashville, TN: Abingdon Press, 1998.

Witherup, Ronald D. *Matthew: God with Us*. Spiritual Commentaries on the Bible. New York: New York City Press, 2000.

www.ingramcontent.com/pod-product-compliance
Lightning Source LLC
Chambersburg PA
CBHW070814100426
42742CB00012B/2357